Pocket CIO – The Guide to Successful IT Asset Management

Get to grips with the fundamentals of IT Asset Management, Software Asset Management, and Software License Compliance Audits with this guide

Phara Estime McLachlan

Pocket CIO – The Guide to Successful IT Asset Management

Copyright © 2018 Packt Publishing

Acquisition Editor: Rebecca Pedley
Content Development Editor: Aditi Gaur
Technical Editor: Prajakta Mhatre
Copy Editor: Safis Editing
Project Coordinator: Suzanne Coutinho
Proofreader: Safis Editing
Production Coordinator: Aparna Bhagat

First published: March 2018
Production reference: 1300318

Published by Packt Publishing Ltd.
Livery Place
35 Livery Street
Birmingham
B3 2PB, UK.

ISBN 978-1-78300-100-2

www.packtpub.com

To my husband, Scott, and wonderful children, Ethan and Ava, who have supported me whole-heartedly through every venture.

`mapt.io`

Mapt is an online digital library that gives you full access to over 5,000 books and videos, as well as industry leading tools to help you plan your personal development and advance your career. For more information, please visit our website.

Why subscribe?

- Spend less time learning and more time coding with practical eBooks and Videos from over 4,000 industry professionals

- Improve your learning with Skill Plans built especially for you

- Get a free eBook or video every month

- Mapt is fully searchable

- Copy and paste, print, and bookmark content

PacktPub.com

Did you know that Packt offers eBook versions of every book published, with PDF and ePub files available? You can upgrade to the eBook version at `www.PacktPub.com` and as a print book customer, you are entitled to a discount on the eBook copy. Get in touch with us at `service@packtpub.com` for more details.

At `www.PacktPub.com`, you can also read a collection of free technical articles, sign up for a range of free newsletters, and receive exclusive discounts and offers on Packt books and eBooks.

Contributors

About the author

Phara Estime McLachlan is a serial entrepreneur, founder, and CEO of Nahteava, a leading management consulting firm specializing in IT and Software Asset Management, advisory services, and innovation. Phara has over 20 years of strategy and operations, innovation and marketing, and technology and consulting experience in the Americas, Asia, and Europe. With two decades of ITSAM experience, Phara works with Fortune 100, mid- to large-size company CIOs, CTOs, CFOs, VPs, asset managers, universities, and public sector agencies (government, city, state agencies) to create holistic IT Asset Management and Software Asset Management programs that close risk gaps, increase productivity, result in cost efficiency, and strengthen cybersecurity.

Prior to founding Nahteava, Phara was the founder and CEO of Animus Solutions, and headed Animus's ITSAM practices, and shaped its strategy and business services. Prior to Animus, Phara consulted independently for some of the Big 4 consulting firms.

For more than a dozen years, Phara has also actively mentored and coached young and experienced IT and software asset managers. Phara is a frequent speaker at conferences and seminars on industry and technology issues and innovation. She's written numerous articles that have appeared in magazines such as Architecture and Governance, Enterprise Apps Today, ITAM Review, CIO Update, Baseline, CRN, CIO.com, ITAK, and many others. Phara strives to share her knowledge and educate those who may be new to the ITAM and SAM industry in any way she can.

In 2012, Phara was named one of the "Next Generation Leaders" by 83 Degrees Online Magazine. Phara has also been recognized as a business leader through awards such as the Business Leaders Top 50 Entrepreneurs in Tampa Bay, PowerBroker Magazine TOP 50—Ranked #18 in Tampa Bay, Southern Business Leader Top Entrepreneurs, Tampa Bay Business Journal Business Woman of the Year Finalist, BizTech Judges Choice Award for CEO of a Technology Company, BizTech Innovation Awards CEO of Technology Company Finalist, Black Enterprise Magazine—Innovator of the Year Finalist, The Stevies - American Business Awards Executive of the Year Finalist.

Phara lives with her husband, Scott, and two wonderful children, Ethan and Ava, in Tampa, Florida.

Packt is searching for authors like you

If you're interested in becoming an author for Packt, please visit authors.packtpub.com and apply today. We have worked with thousands of developers and tech professionals, just like you, to help them share their insight with the global tech community. You can make a general application, apply for a specific hot topic that we are recruiting an author for, or submit your own idea.

Table of Contents

Preface

Anyone at the executive level deals with a plethora of questions and concerns that would make any normal person's head swim. However, those at the C-level cannot afford that, and so they seek answers as a means of ensuring that all is well within the organization. This tactic works until they look at IT. Getting a good, solid answer to the question, "Are we getting a good return on our investment in IT?" is never easy, direct, or straightforward even for many IT managers. Trust us: this situation is commonplace in every industry. Given that a company's IT spend is, next to salary and benefits, the biggest item in the budget, it's almost mindboggling that accountability in this mission critical is so hard to come by. Executives care about the value IT components represent. They long to understand in a concrete manner how IT provides value through cost reductions, new revenue streams, growth opportunities, and compliance.

The credibility of your IT department is at stake if your CIO cannot answer the following seven essential questions:

1. What assets are in place?
2. What return are our assets providing to the business?
3. How are you improving our assets' return?
4. How are our asset investments performing?
5. How are our asset investments performing relative to our competition?
6. Do our assets put our business at risk in any way? Software? Cyber?
7. If so, how are we managing that risk?

In most modern organizations, responsibility for providing these crucial answers falls to the CIO. Still, although ownership of this task is clearly defined, questions still abound:

- How can the performance of IT assets be quantified?
- How can CIOs demonstrate the effective management of IT assets?
- How do CIOs demonstrate that IT provides a solid ROI?
- How do CIOs convey the message that this return is greater than what competitors generate?

The good news is this: there is a way to get the rock-solid answers and evidence every organization must have. ITAM is that way! In this book, I will illustrate exactly how ITAM enables the CIO and their team to answer these important questions. ITAM, which comprises processes, tools, data, and people, manages the entire life cycle of an IT asset (hardware and software). ITAM and SAM best practices allow executives to operate in a predictive manner in terms of what assets the enterprise expects to acquire, as well as what assets it must release.

ITAM not only tracks the costs of every IT asset; it also maps IT assets to business services in a truly meaningful manner. ITAM conveys asset cost information essential to determining the return generated by any given business service. ITAM and SAM help increase those returns through effective vendor and contract management. Lastly, risks associated with IT assets are managed effectively because ITAM and SAM provide insight into vendor warranties and support commitments, software vulnerabilities, entitlements, and asset disposal.

A guide to saving money, making money, and staying in compliance

As a C-level executive and IT and Software Asset Management specialist, I advise and help organizations trying to solve the toughest enterprise issues and reach their peak performance through the most innovative techniques and technology. The *purpose of this book* is to address the burning challenges and questions that all levels in an organization have, such as struggling to implement business practices to manage IT hard and soft assets that result in control, risk reduction, improved compliance, and savings. This book provides specific best practice advice, tools, and examples that can be used to create new or enhance existing programs, and *not provide you with just generic market fluff*. You will be introduced to a variety of approaches that can be used immediately to manage IT Asset Management, Software Asset Management, and Software License Compliance within your organization and work with other programs/processes within your organization, that is, service management, risk, and change.

If you are taking a half-hearted attempt at asset management, you will receive only half the answers you require. ITAM is serious business. This book outlines ITAM and SAM best practices and answers fundamental questions about the ITAM and SAM processes and policies. I know you will find this information helpful in formulating your own ITAM and SAM strategies.

IT and Software Asset Management saves you money by:

- Avoiding penalties for non-compliance
- Keeping projects in house
- Having accurate inventory management
- Accessing a system for reharvest-able software
- Utilizing human capital appropriately
- Minimizing cybersecurity risk

IT and Software Asset Management makes you money by:

- Allowing you to focus on your business
- Running operations efficiently
- Increasing productivity where applied
- Focusing on the future versus the past
- Keeping you ahead of the competition

IT and Software Asset Management keeps you in compliance by:

- Ensuring compliance
- Avoiding penalties for non-compliance
- Understanding liabilities
- Putting processes in place for coverage
- Reducing security risk from unauthorized software within the environment

Who this book is for

This book is intended for CIOs, CTOs, VPs, and asset managers of mid- to large-sized enterprises, organizations, universities, and public sector agencies (government, city, and state agencies). In addition, for individuals responsible for the management of assets within their respective organizations and all users of the organizations IT assets (hardware and software).

If you are dealing with changes such as mergers, acquisitions, divestitures, new products or services, cyber security, mandated regulations, expansion, and much more, this book will help you too.

What this book covers

Chapter 1, *ITAM – It's Not Just IT's Problem or Function*, helps you learn how ITAM affects all aspects of the organization: from profits to legal obligations to operational effectiveness. We will cover how managing IT assets is not just about managing hardware and software within the enterprise, but it's also about how it affects risk exposure, operational inefficiencies, legal obligations, compliance standards, and costs.

Chapter 2, *ITAM Strategy and Plan*, shows how to develop a sound foundation for your ITAM program and explains what ITAM is and isn't. We will also cover the fundamentals and the standard positions of assets at a point in time during the IMACD stages (Install/Move/Add or Change/Disposal), and where in the life cycle process the asset is: control, procure, deploy, manage, or retire.

Chapter 3, *The New Risk Management*, teaches how to govern your ITAM program through policies, processes, and procedures, as well as details and examples of the various types of ITAM policies that you could have and what types of regulations and standards can affect your ITAM and SAM programs, policies, processes, and procedures.

Chapter 4, *What is SAM?*, goes over another key component for ITAM success, Software Asset Management (SAM). You will learn what SAM is, what SAM standards are, how to manage your software assets, and gain an understanding of software contracts. We will also cover license types, usage, contract coverage, and contract reconciliation, and reporting.

Chapter 5, *Understanding and Surviving Software License Compliance Audits*, explains how to survive a software audit and the various steps to take after the traded audit demand letter, email, or phone call arrives.

Chapter 6, *ITAM Tools - What Should You Look For?*, focuses on IT Asset Management tools, ITAM tools strategy, what you should look for in an ITAM tool, and how to determine what your requirements should be. You will also learn what key questions to ask vendors about the tools they are trying to sell.

Chapter 7, *Increasing ITAM Program and Project Success Rates Using Change Management*, covers how change management increases ITAM program and project success. We cover the factors that influence why some projects are successful while others fail, and look for common reasons. The chapter also introduces a way of thinking about projects that is still result oriented, but is equally focused on the people aspect of projects and describes how taking a change management approach to ITAM project success "brings the project to life" for many people and moves them from understanding what is happening to being an active participant in the success of the ITAM project.

Chapter 8, Now What?, explains how to approach your ITAM/SAM program responsibilities, what those responsibilities are exactly, and how to figure out what those responsibilities could be, now that you have implemented and deployed your ITAM/SAM program, policies, and tool.

What you need for this book

This entire book was written as a "how-to" guidebook with specific action-based steps you can take while reading. Keep an open mind. ITAM is dynamic and new regulations, new technologies, and new standards are always being introduced. It is ever changing, which is why you must always be proactive and continuously managing your ITAM/SAM program. As you read through this book, take notes, use the examples, and make them into your own.

Download the color images

We also provide a PDF file that has color images of the screenshots/diagrams used in this book. You can download it here: `https://www.packtpub.com/sites/default/files/downloads/PocketCIOTheGuidetoSuccessfulITAssetManagement_ColorImages.pdf`.

Conventions used

There are a number of text conventions used throughout this book.

Warnings or important notes appear like this.

Tips and tricks appear like this.

Get in touch

Feedback from our readers is always welcome.

General feedback: Email feedback@packtpub.com and mention the book title in the subject of your message. If you have questions about any aspect of this book, please email us at questions@packtpub.com.

Errata: Although we have taken every care to ensure the accuracy of our content, mistakes do happen. If you have found a mistake in this book, we would be grateful if you would report this to us. Please visit www.packtpub.com/submit-errata, selecting your book, clicking on the Errata Submission Form link, and entering the details.

Piracy: If you come across any illegal copies of our works in any form on the Internet, we would be grateful if you would provide us with the location address or website name. Please contact us at copyright@packtpub.com with a link to the material.

If you are interested in becoming an author: If there is a topic that you have expertise in and you are interested in either writing or contributing to a book, please visit authors.packtpub.com.

Reviews

Please leave a review. Once you have read and used this book, why not leave a review on the site that you purchased it from? Potential readers can then see and use your unbiased opinion to make purchase decisions, we at Packt can understand what you think about our products, and our authors can see your feedback on their book. Thank you!

For more information about Packt, please visit packtpub.com.

1
ITAM – It's Not Just IT's Problem or Function

The view of IT has universally evolved from being just another cost center to an important business driver with mission-critical functions. Rapid changes in technology, compliance, and business have created a need to work smarter, more quickly, and with less resources. In the past decade, **IT Asset Management (ITAM)** has been on the forefront for IT executives and executive committee discussions—from cost cutting to increasing efficiencies to better management of the entire operations process. However, the following nagging question remains: what are we getting out of our IT investment?

ITAM must be approached as a key corporate activity that needs executive approval and support, along with planning from finance, human resources, and operations. The primary reasons for this relate to the need to control costs, the increasing importance and complexity of the enterprise's technological infrastructure, and the heightened risk associated with regulatory, cybersecurity, and contractual compliance issues.

As a strategic-level function, ITAM must be aligned with the strategic business plan. The approach must be strategic yet practical, with the recognition that all assets exist to support business services. Simply put, IT assets must be managed throughout their life cycles so as to support business strategy.

Key benefits of ITAM

Success in ITAM requires development of road maps, business cases, practical metrics, time lines, and accountability. Control of IT hardware and software asset costs throughout their life cycles is essential to success.

There are nine key benefits that are derived from ITAM; you should expect all of these outcomes, depending on the scope of your ITAM goals:

- Accountability for assets, services, and their costs
- A road map to best practices
- Practical steps to reach all relevant compliance requirements
- Timely and accurate assessments of future asset needs to meet business and technology initiatives
- An improved position of strength for managing vendors and contracts
- Consistent and proactive software and license management
- Reduced support costs
- Ability to proactively manage **service-level agreements (SLAs)**
- Reduced security risk by highlighting vulnerabilities on unsupported software and noncompliant software instances

What are we getting out of the IT investment?

If your organization cannot easily answer this question, finding the answer should be a high priority. This is where the ITAM process can unlock the answer. ITAM directly affects the effective management of finances. It also brings with it the certainty that IT aligns with—and drives—existing business services. The key to success in ITAM lies in managing IT assets on an enterprise-wide basis and throughout all the respective life cycles. Doing this requires taking a holistic approach and perspective based on the reality that asset management is not just IT's responsibility; everyone shares in it.

The following are the Gartner statistics on benefits of asset management:

- **More highly leveraged buys**: Reduce asset acquisition costs by 5-8%
- **Better matching of software licenses to organization needs**: Reduce software costs by 6-10%
- **Enhanced service and warranty coverage**: Reduce warranty costs by 3-15%
- **Increased component standardization**: Rescue mean-time-to-repair and improve uptime by 3-7%
- **Reduced IT component complexity**: Improve help desk first call resolution rate by 5-12%

- **Better contractor/vendor selection process**: Improve contractor performance by 20%
- **Better negotiation of terms and conditions safeguarding performance**: Reduce risk of noncompliance by 50%
- **Improved asset tracking, proven usage compliance, and ease of audit**: Reduce noncompliance risks by 80-90%

Source: *Jack Heine, Gartner, Gartner Fall Symposium*

The challenge of IT

IT executives have numerous challenges, including the following top four:

- Managing IT as a business
- Aligning the IT infrastructure, projects, and goals to the business priorities
- Finding the budget to meet corporate objectives set by the C-suite
- Meeting compliance in all areas—from industry to financial to IT to cyber

Often, the biggest hurdle, which sums up all of the preceding challenges, is the "do more with less" mandate. Even when profits are up and there is a significant growth, IT budgets don't often grow at the same increased percentage that allows IT to pace with the projects and changes needed in the organization.

ITAM is pivotal to fusing IT with business users. IT assets are supplied and maintained in a manner that facilitates the execution of business goals. Financial accountability and savings through life cycle asset management become a shared success with the business team. ITAM becomes not only the central lynchpin holding together IT, project management, and corporate strategic direction but also the strategic solution that brings IT leaders to the C-level.

Functionally, IT as a business center translates into cost-efficiency while improving service delivery, mitigating risk, and demonstrating business value. As a business process, ITAM has been already working with all the groups enterprise-wide, assisting with or, in some cases, becoming the solution to manage financials, contracts, and business deliverables. The ability to manage targeted assets and tracking the overall inventory and relationships between the assets closes the loop to the operational aspects of IT.

Strategically, ITAM can become the executive dashboard that gives you a holistic view into your organization. ITAM can help identify efficiencies, inefficiencies, and gaps not only in the traditional world of IT, but also in HR, project management, service-oriented functions, and cyber threats.

Cost management

Organizations spend millions of dollars on their IT and operations, sometimes without even knowing where their money is going. From software licensing issues to inefficiencies with the IT service management, the enterprise lose profits without realizing it. There are four culprits within an organization's IT that contribute to huge cost inefficiencies:

- Software
- Hardware
- Downtime
- Distractions of technology

The hidden cost of technology

The following are the hidden cost of technology.

Software

Software controls the total cost of ownership spend. Software ownership is not just about licensing compliance, but it's also about the management of software. During the initial software procurement, there are licensing fees and usages models, contract negotiation fees (for example, lawyers), and implementation. Once you license the asset, there are other considerations, such as follows, and all of them have an associated cost: upgrade and maintenance, shelf-ware, software support, and IT training.

Added to software are the typical over- or under-licensed issues, which usually account for an increased 30%, on average, but can result in a potential loss of millions. Dependent on the size and scope of the software "gap," an organization could double its unnecessary software spend by the end of year three when annual maintenance fees are accounted for. While an initial discovery could uncover these cost savings, unless it is managed with a robust software asset management program and governed by a strict procurement policy, unexpected software costs soar and become excessive.

Hardware

While **hardware** is an expected capital cost, the lifetime cost for repair and maintenance of a single PC is as high as $2,162.89*. There is also the additional $128.09 attributed to the loss of productivity incurred per user per PC due to unforeseen downtime, such as shutdowns, reboots, and hours. If you view the cost based on 5,000 PCs or 5,000 users, that's over 10 million spent on the average life of those PCs. Assuming 4 years as the average life cycle, those 5,000 machines cost 2.5 million every year. Add the loss productivity cost, and that's another $160,000 annually.

With many organizations, hardware asset management discussions also include servers, RACs, mobile devices, and the like. With on-premise servers, a number of areas need to be reviewed for those hidden costs, as follows:

- What license is required?
- What are the limitations of the licensing based on the server?
- How many cores does the server have?
- What is the server used for?
- What is on the server?

Cloud and hardware: We can't ignore cloud services, the elephant in the room, when talking about hardware. Ironically, with cloud services being sold as "not needing additional hardware," the reality is that cloud does need hardware—servers to be precise—in the backend. Cloud needs not only servers but also a physical space. While that doesn't seem to apply to your organization, it does because you still need software and then the questions start coming in. Who is licensing the software? Who is responsible? Does the licensing change? Where does the software license reside?

I could probably write a small book about the ironies of cloud, but, in all likelihood, you've heard it ad nauseam if cloud options were explored any given time in the past few years.

Critical downtime leads to lost revenue

Large organizations, defined as those with more than 2,500 users, have increased their average downtime by 69% from 8.7 to 14.7 hours per month**. Downtime due to failed technology is one of the main culprits in cost inefficiency.

A total of 44% of organizations surveyed by Osterman Research and Electric Cloud estimated that the last significant software bug resulted in an average of $250,000 in lost revenue in 20 developer hours to correct it. The increase of an incorrect technology use or a failed technology exposes all organizations to risks such as downtime on critical applications.

The distractions of technology

With the Internet, it is easy to just check on one thing. The issue of social media and digital entertainment can truly become a crippling factor to productivity. In a recent survey of Britain's 34 million-person workforce, 6% spend more than 1 hour on social media while at work, translating to $22.16 billion in lost annual revenue**. The distractions of technology, such as Facebook, Twitter, and other social media networks, and iTunes, YouTube, and general digital entertainment kills productivity. Social and digital media at work causes countless interruptions during the day and results in operational inefficiencies and lost revenue.

Your answer may be to block certain apps and sites, but the truth is that technology distractions continue on with mobile phones and other mobile devices. At least if you allow the site on user terminals, your organization can monitor the amount of time spent on these sites and the best method to address this issue.

Cost control mechanisms

Cost control, also known as cost management or cost-containment, can, and should, be used as a method to improve business cost efficiencies, and it helps to reduce costs.

Understand that your organization is constantly and consistently seeking cost and operational efficiencies, regardless of economic conditions. View cost control in a holistic fashion—from the view of your executive team, the CFO, COO, and the CIO/CTO. Your team should comprise people with expertise in finance, IT, and operations from a variety of backgrounds. Regard cost control as the nexus for your entire organization.

*According to Gartner
**According to Harris Interactive

Why manage IT assets?

A vast many organizations choose to either not manage their IT assets or only manage part of their assets. Many who attempt ITAM are usually only taking physical inventory or just doing a cursory software license discovery process in preparation for an audit. Although these processes are better than nothing, and they certainly have their place, they do not offer the insight and clarity required to determine the return on your organization's IT spend. Only an organizational commitment to manage IT resources in a holistic enterprise approach can help you achieve that. Also, again, ITAM can, and should, be used as a corporate strategy.

If you are looking for good reasons to start managing IT assets more effectively, consider these:

- **Cost**: In IT and business, change is a constant, and along with every change comes a cost. Typically, the upfront purchase or investment in technology accounts for roughly 4% to 20% of those costs. The remainder is spread over the entire life cycle of your IT assets. These costs include equipment (including software installation), managing changes, maintenance, upgrades, virtualization, service or help desk setup and maintenance, and disposal. Arriving at an accurate figure for the cost of your IT assets is a challenge. Additionally, getting the most out of your IT infrastructure investment is virtually impossible when there is no accurate record of the organization's IT assets and how they are supporting critical business services.

- **Dependency**: IT enables your business to operate globally on a 24x7 basis. Given this, your IT infrastructure is too important to be left unmanaged. ITAM should play an important role, adding value to your organization's growth strategies. However, uncovering this role requires a clear understanding of the relationships and dependencies involved with these mission-critical assets.

- **Hardware replacement (technology refresh)**: Whether you like it or not, the pressure to stay competitive is going to drive you to replace IT hardware assets every 3 years. Given that today's hardware has a 3-year "life" before it becomes obsolete, this is a reasonable expectation. Also, if a major shift in technology develops, you may find yourself replacing your entire array of hardware assets.

How does ITAM help?

When it comes to achieving cost savings and increased efficiencies and maintaining regulatory compliance of your IT assets, ITAM is essential, but as a strategic initiative, a sound ITAM strategy enables you to accomplish the following objectives:

- Accurate asset tracking
- Effective IT asset management
- Effective software asset management
- Efficient asset disposal
- Timely asset replacement
- Risk mitigation (for example, around software compliance, patch management, antivirus, and many more)
- Cost reduction

However, ITAM involves more than accomplishing these objectives. Your strategy must be broad enough and sound enough to include other necessary asset management objectives, such as contract management, license compliance, and IT financial management.

Historically, hardware assets were "written off" when they reached obsolescence. However, today's hardware assets hold considerably more value, even when replaced. Before an asset can be evaluated, it must first be located and assessed. When dealing with a leased equipment, it's wise to remember that the aim is to return the assets by the negotiated end of the lease agreement, thereby avoiding costly penalties. Here, the challenge is to quickly locate the equipment that has been in use for some time, but may have never been tracked. A fundamental aspect of ITAM is tracking the location of each hardware asset all the time. Therefore, no matter how the equipment is acquired—either through purchase or lease—effective ITAM practices enhance cost efficiencies.

Tracking the flow of software throughout your organization can also be a challenge. Best practices are all well and good, but the consistent application of those practices is the key. Remember, compliance is about meeting and maintaining audit-ready status all the time, not only when the audit time rolls around.

Most businesses succeed in logging the first user of their software or equipment, but fail to track the changes that occur during the normal course of business. These include routine items such as the installation or deinstallation of software, applying necessary patches, adding memory, installing a larger hard disk, or reassigning the asset to a different user.

The failure to track any of these changes frequently results in a lost, unlicensed asset, hacking and security breaches. An asset management solution that does not track these changes is not a solution at all.

Other information worth tracking includes contract information, such as leasing/replacement dates, insurance contracts, maintenance agreements, and software license agreements. These types of data are invaluable to ITAM because they provide insight and accuracy into the costs associated with these items. This in turn provides you with clarity when it comes down to deciding whether to purchase or lease a specific equipment. Although lease rates may look attractive initially, your total cost for that lease may actually end up exceeding the cost of purchasing the equipment outright. Remember that 3 years into the lease, you may be paying for obsolete equipment, and those rates lose some of their luster.

In a nutshell, building the discipline required to make ITAM work for your enterprise results in the following benefits:

- Ensuring compliance
- Maintaining audit readiness
- Effectively managing service costs
- Maintaining your competitive edge
- Enhancing operational productivity
- Ability for IT to respond to vulnerabilities in a timely manner
- Implementing consistent and repeatable processes
- Reducing the cost of change
- Managing asset utilization
- Releasing capital
- Improving bottom-line profitability
- Increasing organizational ability to meet service-level agreements
- Improving customer satisfaction
- Managing financial accountability for IT
- Collaboration with IT Security to discover possible and unknown cyber threats

Implementing ITAM within your organization leads to faster and greater success to existing and new initiatives. The following table provides a sample list of key CIO initiatives and shows how leveraging ITAM enables a more proactive approach:

CIO initiatives	IT Asset Management enablement	Executive team interest
Cloud computing	Cost versus benefit analysis with accurate understanding of all assets required for a function that might be moved to the cloud	• Greater efficiency and control at the enterprise level
Service-Oriented Architecture (SOA)	Usage data allows consolidation, reduced maintenance costs, and alignment with business	• Significantly reduced cost center • Business intelligence • Performance measurement • Security
Compliance	Managed software list, snapshots of current system configurations, and document management	• Cost control • Compliance
Service management	Continual updates of asset data, usage, costs, users, populating service management incident, problem, change, and asset management	• Improved productivity • Reduction in resources dedicated to this function • Ability to bring business back to home nation
Vendor management	Manage approved vendor list, manage terms and conditions, reduce risk, and evaluate vendors	• Cost savings and align IT financials enterprise-wide • Reduction in risk • Compliance
Manage IT as part of the business	Align investment with business priorities, analyze financial opportunities for savings, and evaluate Provide a snapshot of current system configurations for compliance and capacity planning	• Savings all around from financial to other resources • Greater flexibility during business changes
Legacy systems integration	Impact assessment, cost versus benefit, and data capture	• Cost savings that are unimaginable

Security and risk management	Identify suspicious configurations, enforce standards, and highlight vulnerabilities on unsupported software and noncompliant software instances	• IT Security • Cyber Security • Network Security • Behavior-based Security • Social Engineering

Why finance executives need to pay attention

Misalignment between finance and IT is a common problem in many organizations, giving rise to a long-standing debate about just how involved finance executives need to be with the IT department. Both departments have the same goal, that is, operational efficiencies throughout the organization that will keep costs down.

So why is there so often a lack of alignment? Why do these two functions seem to be working against each other?

The reality is that IT and finance are two very different organisms. They work differently, talk differently, and think differently. In fact, they have very little in common, aside from their goals. They are apples and oranges.

A perfect example of this divide is the differing approaches to a very important aspect of an organization's IT function: ITAM. To the finance side of the house, ITAM means short-term cost savings. Period. Never mind even if that can lead to penny-wise/dollar-foolish decisions!

Finance executives most certainly should be paying attention to the ITAM program. Although they don't need to know the ins and outs of the actual program, financial executives will care about the bottom line: ITAM programs that can garner as much as 20% overall organizational savings annually.

What makes ITAM so important?

There are countless reasons why ITAM is important or should be important to any organization. First and foremost, ITAM touches on all aspects of an organization—anywhere from small projects to corporate compliance and everything in-between. Anything that can touch upon all aspects of an organization has to be vitally important. With ITAM, we've only just begun our journey. ITAM is still a maturing practice, but the following are some common critical factors that make ITAM important:

- **Compliance**: Compliance, whether it's with software vendors or with government regulators, is a key issue for any organization. Noncompliance means one thing, huge costs—fines, fees, and, in some cases, even jail time, not to mention bad PR. All of these things cost an organization dearly. ITAM is an efficient way to keep track of all of your IT assets so that you always know what you have, where it is deployed, and who is using it. When the auditors come calling, you will be better prepared to answer their questions and have a better understanding of your levels of compliance. Being unprepared is never a good option.

- **IT asset lifecycle**: IT assets, be it software, hardware, or mobile assets, are the lifeblood of an organization in today's world. Managing their life cycle efficiently can bring cost savings to your organization. For example, if a piece of hardware is no longer performing as it should be, it could actually hinder productivity and cost you money every minute it's in use. Constant evaluation of your assets and their performance is a great way to keep everything running at its optimal level and keeping productivity up at all times.

- **Expense management**: IT assets and their maintenance come with a cost, typically as much as 20% of the IT budget annually. In order to keep that line item on the expense report to a minimum, properly managing your assets can help in many ways—from ensuring that assets are properly retired to reconciling your equipment against fees. For example, are you paying for assets that you aren't using? When employees come and go, is there a process in place to reassign their cellphone, laptop, and other equipment? In a large organization, with constant changes on a large scale, lack of a process can mean big expenses for idle assets.

- **Security**: When you think of ITAM, security isn't usually something that comes to mind, but it should. A successful ITAM program can mean increased security and decreased risk. How? For starters, consider that virtually every employee has a computer at home, some of them company-issued. How do you keep track of what they are downloading or sharing when they are outside of the office? If they don't vpn, how are you ensuring that they are getting the necessary patches? You may be pushing out to all assets connected to the network. A solid set of IT policies and procedures can control the level of security risk your organization is exposed to simply by setting limits. Another way to think of security is the collaboration between ITAM and the IT Security team. Your security team can leverage the data that ITAM has collected to proactively identify known software vulnerabilities. IT security will be able to assess the assets that pose a threat to your organization. They will know where the assets are located, view software, install data, and the business service it is tied to. This is all possible by having ITAM in place.

- **Software contract management**: With most organizations in a constant state of change, managing software contracts is often overlooked. The finance department needs to understand that there are significant cost savings to be had simply by paying close attention to terms and conditions and renegotiating when the time calls for it. Additionally, with vendors changing their rules as frequently as they do, not being on top of your terms and conditions can equal noncompliance, and we know what that means! Suppose that your organization has just opened an office in London, and your IT department ships them preloaded laptops to use, but nobody checked your software licensing agreement. Your terms and conditions don't include transferability. Software licenses generally limit transferability. Lack of transferability increases the cost of divestiture, requiring additional licensing for the divested company and creating a glut of additional licenses for the retained companies. Additional licensing terms, including pricing, may be less favorable for the divested company, further increasing the divestiture costs. If the divested company owns the contract and licenses without transferability, the divested company may be stuck with a glut of licenses and create a gap and licensing requirement for retained entities covered by the contracts licenses. This is just one example of how organizations can fall out of compliance, resulting in additional hefty fees and penalties.

- **IT service management**: IT isn't just something that affects employees; it affects everyone touched by your organization, from vendors to customers. Any finance executive worth their salt can see how a failure in IT can directly affect the bottom line. On the flip side, having a solid performing IT department will result in a better experience for everyone, including customers. The degree to which IT affects the customer service will vary according to industry, but it will have an effect.

Tips for a positive working relationship – on both sides

Now you understand a little more about why ITAM is so important to both the bottom line and top line. However, the following question remains: how can finance get involved?

I have a few suggestions for how finance and IT can work better together; the first step is simply realizing just how much they need each other!:

1. **Schedule recurring meetings**: Finance should always know what is going on with IT, and vice versa. Monthly or even quarterly update meetings will be mutually beneficial for both parties. Discuss new projects coming up, new initiatives being taken, and use each other to help accelerate your mutual goals. This should also be an opportunity for the finance team to check in on projects that they have previously approved. Most executives approve a budget and leave it at that. Both parties should always be in the know regarding ongoing and even completed projects.

2. **Always consult the tech guys**: IT is usually brought in at the last minute when more software licenses or hardware are needed due to a large business change. This is a big mistake. When IT is given the chance to plan ahead, they have a greater leverage and potential to save money for the organization. Last minute decisions will end up costing more in the short and long term. Bring in the IT department from the beginning, and make it a collaborative process.

3. **Make ITAM a priority, for everyone**: I have explained how ITAM can equal significant cost savings. The next step is getting buy in across the organization. An ongoing ITAM program needs to be on everyone's priority list in order for it to work. This includes the C-Suite. An alignment between the finance and IT departments is an important step, but in order to keep the project going, it's important that these two departments work together to keep the rest of the organization in the same mindset.

Implementing an effective ITAM program within your organization is a positive step toward lowering risk, increasing compliance, and creating optimal efficiency. The marriage between finance and IT is imperative to its success. Marriages are never perfect, so you can expect some bumps along the way. However, working in tandem, with open lines of communication, is in the best interests of the organization and, more importantly, the bottom line.

Building the case for ITAM

We will build the case for ITAM using the following ways.

Leadership

Over 50% of senior executives feel that improving the overall quality of their organization's leadership is a critical challenge, and 46% believe they must do a better job of developing the next generation of leaders, increasing employee commitment, and retaining top talent.*

*Sources:

- Global CEO Study, Booze Allen Hamilton
- 2009 Duke University Executive Leadership Survey

"We live and work in a world where organizational failure is endemic, and where frank, comprehensive dissections of those failures are still woefully infrequent; where success is too easily celebrated and failures are too quickly forgotten; where short-term earnings and publicity concerns block us from confronting, much less learning from our stumbles and our blunders."

– Jena McGregor, Fast Company Magazine, February 2005

The best companies, as measured by innovation, profitability, growth, reputation, and long-term track record, always seem to have the best leaders—not just at the top, but also at every management level throughout the enterprise. This is not an accident. These are companies with senior leaders who understand how to get the best from themselves and their people. They understand that their most valuable resource is not products, capital, or real estate, but people. They know that good people led by outstanding leaders is what separates great organizations from the rest.

Leadership is not about luck

Understand that good leadership doesn't have to be a question of luck, and it certainly isn't magic. Leadership is a business skill like any other, the most important business skill of all. Work with mentor individuals, management teams, and larger groups to increase their leadership skills. Help them understand the dynamics of individual and organizational leadership. This is a proven delivery system for better thinking, smarter decisions, effective communication, motivated employees, and ultimately, better top-line and bottom-line business results.

Great leadership enables the following:

- Attracting and retaining top talent
- Motivating your workforce
- Shaping the personality and reputation of your organization
- Generating value from outsourced relationships
- Organizational change
- Employee awareness and communications

You must be thinking, what does leadership have to do with ITAM and building the case for ITAM?

Virtually, every enterprise of any size talks about ITAM strategy, but how many have successfully integrated it into their IT culture? The evidence suggests only about a third: in 2009, only 32% of IT projects started were completed successfully; another 44 % were considered partial failures, and 24% were considered complete failures.* A batting average of 0.320 might be terrific in Major League Baseball, but no business enterprise should accept such a paltry success rate.

There were many reasons cited for this dismal record of IT failure, such as lack of user input, lack of technical competence, changing requirements or specifications, lack of C-suite support, the economy, lack of resources, obsolescence, poor communication, the list goes on. In fact, all of these factors and many more would become moot, or nearly so, with a comprehensive ITAM strategy in place supported and led by strong leaders/champions of the ITAM program.

A good ITAM strategy starts with expert analysis of organizational needs, followed by C-suite buy in, which likes the operational efficiencies and cost savings over time. A well-designed ITAM strategy also makes the most of available resources, identifies technology and software needs based on business objectives and existing IT portfolios, and makes allowances for company growth and evolving technology requirements.

Source: 2009 CHAOS Report on IT project success rates, published by The Standish Group, Boston.

The approach starts by asking key questions; here, you will learn what questions to ask, where to go to find the answers you need to help you build the case, and the answer to the hard question of how will ITAM benefit the business:

- What are the corporate goals? Check the company newsletter, town halls, presentations by the CEO, or the information for shareholders on the company website.
- What objective is your competition for budget, and does that objective have a stronger link to the corporate goals? If the link is stronger, you can choose to rework your priorities to a stronger case yourself, or you may choose to dovetail your objectives to the other. For instance, if a health-care system is faced with allocating funds between new imaging equipment and improvements for managing assets, propose reducing the need for redundant portable equipment through improvements in your asset-tracking project request.
- Have you sought external validation? Researching analyst and vendor white papers, and extracting relevant statistics and comments, takes the personal aspects out from your project request. Check out trends by reviewing headlines over a few weeks in technology and industry websites.
- Have you sought internal validation? Talk to peers and managers in other end departments and listen to their ideas. If you don't have internal numbers to back up your project request, perform a survey or a random inventory and report the findings.
- Have you increased the visibility of the good work you and your team have done already (savings, customer satisfaction, and so on) and highlighted the failures to be corrected in the requested budgeted project?

Look for strategic IT opportunities that will help you to build your case and strengthen a positive outcome to bringing ITAM to your organization. The following are a few examples to help you get started:

- **Software audits**: Audits by software companies and by compliance agencies are on the rise. Waiting to receive a letter leaves no options for reducing the number of licenses or buying licenses at non-crisis pricing. Can you prove the right to use? Understanding what information you need to keep and what choices you have during negotiations all deliver to the bottom line and to feeding accurate data for strategic planning.

- **Acquisition/mergers**: IT executives have an important role in determining the cost of integrating a new acquisition into the organization. The level of detail necessary to do the job right requires ITAM. Take advantage of software consolidation rather than be trapped with unexpected expenses. Regulatory compliance is scrutinized intensely during and after an acquisition. Manage this risk with the proper information.

- **Technology to drive innovation**: Technology certainly enables the business of the organization, but it can also make a difference in market leadership. When executives make a critical choice, it can provide the information they need to assess the advantages and disadvantages accurately. The "devil" in the details is an ITAM program that cannot deliver this critical information when needed.
- **Profitability**: To be part of the business, IT assets must deliver the expected value and facilitate achievement of business goals. Executives are accountable to shareholders and to industry regulators. Tax requirements, depreciation, and the value of corporate assets can all be verified or their accuracy can be improved by comparison to the tactical ITAM data.

Tactical goals drive the achievement of strategic goals. Group tactical actions and processes into objectives and begin to relate upwards. Here, you will learn some key objectives and their related actions and processes:

Managing the life cycle	• Inventory tracking • Meet service-level agreements • Maximize ROI from asset investment • Build the data necessary for ITAM and CMDB, tactical, and strategic reporting • Automate essential components
Managing costs	• Eliminate over-licensing of software • Monitor usage to eliminate unused software • Standards offer volume purchasing and a higher rate of reuse • Reduce loss through enforced policies • Manage leases and increase rate of return • Redeploy where cost efficient • Review warranties and maintenance against actual assets and usage
Improving service	• Streamline and consolidate service offerings with accuracy • Increase visibility of nonperforming assets, vendors, or departments • Integrate systems to reduce data errors and duplication of effort

Supporting other initiatives	• Provide updated information to disaster recovery and contingency planning programs • Reduce variability in environment to enhance security efforts • Increase visibility of assets to aid in compliance for Sarbanes Oxley, HIPAA, and other regulations • Improve customer privacy through policy enforcement of asset use, maintenance, and configuration • Support green efforts by buying energy-saving hardware and through imposing sleep settings
Managing risk	• Meet compliance objectives of transparent chains of automation • Mitigate risk of over/underutilized software by comparing owned licenses to discovered software • Address regulatory concerns by maintaining proof-of use documentation • Reduce liability in partner/vendor relationships by managing contractual obligations • Develop employee awareness programs for policies and security issues and assess the ramifications
Providing decision support	• Analyze the hardware reliability and serviceability • Evaluate vendors • Develop catalogs of assets by service • Build proactive loss and theft prevention programs • Evaluate software usage prior to renewal • Develop and deliver budget/chargeback reporting • Deliver cost savings reports • Deliver feedback to negotiators, procurement on choices

Management No-Go on ITAM

ITAM is rarely seen as a strategic initiative at the moment, but those few forward-thinking companies that have tied in ITAM as a strategic initiative have started to reap the benefits. Creating and implementing an ITAM initiative is daunting as the likelihood of seeing the benefits over time will bear significant results, but after the initial first *big success*, the successes over the first year to 18 months after that are more modest, as the ITAM initiative needs constant care and feeding.

Unfortunately, ITAM is often one of the first items to be shut down when an organization hits a rough patch. In these cases, the organizations see ITAM as a nonessential activity, which is in fact not the case. Organizations often end up making decisions that are often shortsighted with a big impact on the long-term health of the company or even industry. Take Microsoft as an example and consider its long wait to get into mobility. That's only one example, but there are so many others to draw upon. It is not the first time IT has teetered on the brink of this particular dilemma, and on more than one occasion, the crows have come home to roost.

In the course *Converting Strategy into Action* offered by Stanford University, they emphasize the importance of understanding the culture and the structure of a company as a critical input in moving ideas from a vision to a practical solution and indicate that these same aspects have a direct bearing on the adoption and success rates of the endeavors of a company.

ITAM will, but management isn't buying – points to demonstrate value of an ITAM program

The value from asset management comes from the following two areas:

- Reduced cost or improved asset utilization
- Reduced risk

There are many other measures, components, and processes that make up asset management, but only value and risk will be seen and understood by the executives paying the bills for these services.

Unless your ITAM program can automatically calculate certain KPAs, processes, or SLAs, you can compare reports on several topics, such as asset reallocation, budget savings, reducing gaps between purchased licenses and those installed, and the time it took to accomplish those tasks with or without your program; you can then evaluate approximately the return on investment and how much it brings to your company. It also depends on the number of employees and how segmented your asset management team is. Analyzing your workflow processes for each employee might shed some light on unnecessary tasks within your department, and that would represent an opportunity to improve productivity.

For some, the low hanging fruit is really more around the OPEX cost reduction aspects of ITAM; ROI becomes the logical result.

Some look at the ongoing cost centers—such as ITSM, ERP, procurement and disposal, Energy, and HRIS—and then specific intermittent projects—such as M and A activity, software compliance, OP systems upgrades, and datacenter consolidation and virtualization—for which the value of having a dynamic and up-to-date ITAM system in place is invaluable. An operating system upgrade project alone in a mid to large company may justify the cost of ITAM systems and personnel for many months or years to come.

In Murphy's law, knowing oneself is the ultimate form of aggression. Similarly, in ITAM, knowing where you are broken exposes the value in the ITAM process:

- Does your ITSM system work from live data?
- Is the ERP fixed asset reconciled with the ITAM repository?
- Do you manage software purchases and landscape to the extent that you know your license position (entitlements versus deployments). (Each copy out of compliance can represent $150,000 in fines).
- Do you know how much IT assets are deployed, where they are, their configuration, and the status of these assets?
- Are you aware of what's being disposed of, how it is recorded, and whether software is being harvested for reuse?

From a cost standpoint, if you cannot answer these questions, you might consider this one guiding fact: cost reduction could easily approach 12%-15% of the overall IT budget, no kidding. This alone justifies a good well-funded ITAM function year after year.

One of the main focuses needed for ITAM is to show that it can reduce cost and provide metrics. You can do this in the software management space by reducing renewal costs and standardizing software. Other significant areas of ITAM that can bear results are as follows:

- Reduction in cyber security risk by highlighting vulnerabilities on unsupported software and noncompliant software instances
- Tracking disposal of machines and providing verification of asset status in an automated method

Although all the points just mentioned are accurate, executive management will not move forward if presented with *what can be* versus *what it is* along with some type of data and reasons for making ITAM a top priority. Often, executive management will look at other priorities as the *real* priorities, especially in the face of a financial crisis, cyber attack, or an industry upset.

The top priority for companies is ensuring the relevancy of their offerings. The next priorities are fulfillment of those lines of business, increasing market share, and providing value to their customers. The underlying factor is the need companies have for mobility, social media, fostering an innovative culture, and leveraging their employees' entrepreneurial spirit in addition to finding talent that is knowledgeable and experienced with all the new technologies and nontraditional ways of engaging people to want a company over its competitors.

Why is this relevant to ITAM? How does it demonstrate the value of the ITAM program? Looking at the priorities of the company, an ITAM program can/may do the following things:

- Create funding for programs through its cost savings from the ITAM program or by leveraging the existing technology for new initiatives (without having to purchase).
- Time efficiency will increase employee productivity by creating an automated process that fosters employees to be innovative and agile with the ability to brainstorm creatively. ITAM eliminates the constant *firefighting mode* at work and creates a more proactive, preventive maintenance mode.
- It may align IT with business to create a collaborative environment, resulting in a profit center. How is this achieved? With ITAM, IT has a 360-degree view that creates transparency in all areas and stages of the business. ITAM helps manage the full life cycle. Although not everything on that cycle falls under IT, ITAM opens the door for communication. IT now has a clearer picture of what the company needs and its pain points. This strategy can lead companies to go to market faster in an accelerated execution phase.

These are some of the key points presented and may prove to be of value to executive management and lead them to move forward and provide the much needed support to their ITAM and SAM teams. With SAM, use these points, among others, plus some scary real-world events, for buy-in on the ITAM program.

Get funded in a bad budget year

During the 2008 financial crisis, enterprise IT groups worldwide had a dire warning and expectations of a great budget reduction. This is no surprise, as any bad year for a company or even an industry leads to decreased funding. During any crisis year, the business case for ITAM must be compelling and relevant.

The following are some steps that best demonstrate the value of that IT improvement business case:

First, avoid focusing solely on financial savings. In a squeezed budget year, it would seem natural for IT managers to promote the direct and indirect savings that are expected from the project. Although outlining the savings is absolutely expected, focusing on that one goal may reduce your chances for approval and funding. Ask yourself how this project relates to corporate and CIO-specific goals. How can you present the value of the project in relation to those goals? Unless you can answer this question and include it in your business case, it is unlikely that you will be funded.

Second, avoid stating benefits solely from an IT operational perspective. A business case that does not lay out the benefits to customers (internal and external) is unlikely to win the funding contest. Certainly, operational improvements will occur when the project is completed. Will the CIO be able to figure out the global value of risk reduction of loss or theft if you only explain the expected improvements in the life-cycle process?

Stepping back from the heads-down detailed view to analyze the global value can be the hardest part of preparing a business case. You cannot assume that the executives have done research on or can intuit how the project relates to their ultimate goals. You have to create those connections for the executive team in a crystal clear manner.

To assure that your project receives a proper review and is compared at full value with other possible budget items, consider taking the following steps before hitting send on that business case:

1. **Relate the project to how it will help the company grow**: Companies acquire, merge, and divest often to increase profitability. While the deal on paper is good, the advantages gained can be lost in the execution of how assets are controlled and inventoried. Acquiring a company with inadequate software licenses, a pending audit, or software licenses that are not transferable is a nightmare. Can the business case relate how these improvements prepare the organization for a major change? Can the documentation developed during the project be added to the due diligence team's materials so that they can analyze a prospective acquisition accordingly?

2. **Understand the CIO's personal and corporate goals**: If the CIO is a heads down IT-focused leader, then a business case built on savings from efficiency may still work. However, CIOs are less internally focused because operational goals do not lead to a seat on the executive team. The upwardly mobile CIO ties IT department activities to corporate goals such as increasing profitability or customer satisfaction. A business case that presents upgrading to maintain technology is more likely to be funded if it is related to a corporate goal such as solving a specific business issue.

3. **Always include service management**: The service management approach to IT operations is popular and is frequently reported in the media read by executives. If an IT project will help improve the execution of a service or the adoption of service management principles, then ensure that you explicitly state how the change will lead to enhanced service management.

4. **Relate projects to impending technology changes**: Sometimes, a major project that has been already underway is the most important aspect to mention in the business case. If the business case can be construed as competing against money already spent, you have already lost. However, if you can show how this project adds value to the ongoing project, you gain a perception advantage and champion those who are invested in the success of the other project. For example, the adoption of virtualized servers changes the relationship of the server to the cost center, eliminating one per application or department. What if an automation project business case lists that the configurations and inventory will be easily tracked in a virtual environment as a benefit? Surely, the business case is much more likely to snag attention than if it was focused on the goal of improving control of the asset inventory.

5. **Uncover "found money"**: A business case must always talk about the cost versus benefit to be considered at all. In many cases, IT projects can offer a reasonable expectation of savings based on expenditures that will not occur, enabling bulk purchasing or freeing up resources through automation. Ensure that the savings are real and measurable. Sampling is a reasonable method for gauging the potential savings. Other sources of information to back up predicted savings can come from research on the Internet, analysts, or even your vendors, who are eager to help you receive funding.

By stepping away from the details and relating the project to external influences, the project is more likely to be understood and weighed appropriately against other initiatives.

Summary

ITAM affects all aspects of the enterprise, from profits to legal obligations to operational effectiveness.

Just as a cutting-edge technology or services can drive a company's earnings, mismanagement of its assets and operations can erode profits, no matter how substantial. Managing IT assets is not just about managing hardware and software within the enterprise, but it's also about how it effects risk exposure, operational inefficiencies, legal obligations, compliance standards, and costs. Failure to manage IT assets effectively can result in legal liabilities and proceedings, financial reporting errors, hefty fines associated to industry legislation, and excess spending of financial and human capital. Companies can save up to 30% in management costs per asset in the first year, according to Gartner Inc., and an effective asset management program can reduce their total cost of ownership by 10% to 15%, on average.

In the end, and right here at the beginning, you must understand that managing an asset effectively requires understanding the total costs associated with the asset. Understanding how the asset supports business critical services throughout its life span is also crucial. It is vitally important to ensure that you have both an accurate analysis and understanding of the costs associated with budgeting, allocation, accounting, and service valuation for every asset. Determining IT's true return on investment without this information is not doable.

Answering the following five fundamental questions provides a snapshot of the effectiveness of your current asset management strategy, assuming that you have one:

- What IT assets are in your possession?
- Do these assets support the profitability of your business?
- How do these assets support your business?
- How much is it costing your business to maintain these assets?
- Is the return worth the cost?

Only a fraction of organizations have reached maturity in ITAM, the level where processes designed for best practices are in place and continually improve the strategic alignment, cost effectiveness, and integration of IT assets. You are now equipped to define the challenges you face and organize and build a consensus for change. In the next chapter, you will learn how to create your ITAM strategy and plan.

2
ITAM Strategy and Plan

Asset management is an evolutionary process, and one that is essential in the development of your organization. Your enterprise will never achieve the level of excellence you envision without the development and implementation of key management processes, of which ITAM is one. Adopting a planned, holistic approach to integrating ITAM into your organizational functions and flow helps make the transition more stable, providing your organization with the most benefit in the most efficient manner.

Are you ready for the evolution?

An honest, objective self-assessment is the best way to understand your maturity level of where you are right now in relation to ITAM, as well as where you want to go. Keep in mind that assessments of this type often benefit from the assistance of outside consultants, those whose interests coincide with the best interests of your organization. Lastly, remember that self-acceptance of the self-assessment results is really the start of your journey toward excellence in ITAM disciplines.

As an aid in your decision making, here is my adaption of the *Process Maturity Model for IT Asset Management 2003* from Gartner, which is one of the most popularly cited maturity models across ITAM literature:

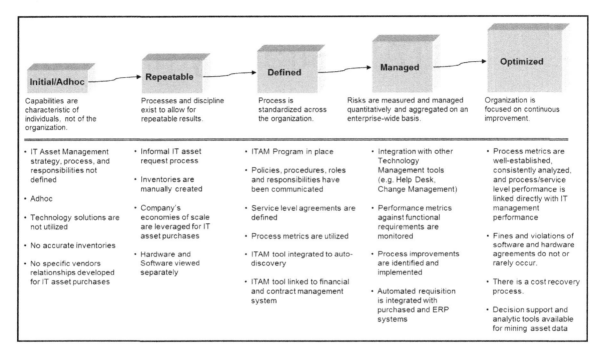

The following screenshot illustrates where your organization is at a point in time. You should define what stage you are when you begin, at a mid-point and at the end:

ITAM Program Maturity – Month + Year					
Acquisition Management	Initial/Adhoc	Repeatable	Defined	Managed	Optimized
Asset Identification	Initial/Adhoc	Repeatable	Defined	Managed	Optimized
Communication & Education Management	Initial/Adhoc	Repeatable	Defined	Managed	Optimized
Compliance Management	Initial/Adhoc	Repeatable	Defined	Managed	Optimized
Disposal Management	Initial/Adhoc	Repeatable	Defined	Managed	Optimized
Documentation Management	Initial/Adhoc	Repeatable	Defined	Managed	Optimized
Financial Management	Initial/Adhoc	Repeatable	Defined	Managed	Optimized
Legislation Management	Initial/Adhoc	Repeatable	Defined	Managed	Optimized
Policy Management	Initial/Adhoc	Repeatable	Defined	Managed	Optimized
Program Management	Initial/Adhoc	Repeatable	Defined	Managed	Optimized
Project Management	Initial/Adhoc	Repeatable	Defined	Managed	Optimized
Vendor Management	Initial/Adhoc	Repeatable	Defined	Managed	Optimized

The following are a few more points to aid you in determining your organizations maturity level:

Stage 1: In the initial/adhoc stage, an organization is at what some would call the chaotic organization where:

- Capabilities are characteristic of individuals, not of the organization
- ITAM strategy, process, and responsibilities are not defined
- Technology solutions are not utilized
- There are no accurate inventories
- There are no specific vendors relationships developed for IT asset purchases
- There are no way of measuring exposures or risks

Stage 2: In the repeatable stage, an organization is at what some would call the reactive organization where:

- Processes and discipline exist to allow for repeatable results
- Informal IT asset request process
- Inventories are manually created
- The company's economies of scale are leveraged for IT asset purchases
- The discovery tool functions as the ITAM tool

Stage 3: In the defined stage, an organization is at what some would call the proactive organization where:

- The process is standardized across the organization
- An ITAM program is in place
- Policies, procedures, roles, and responsibilities have been communicated
- Service-level agreements are defined
- Process metrics are utilized
- The ITAM/SAM tool is integrated to auto-discovery
- The ITAM/SAM tool effectively integrates and reconciles to contractual and financial information, providing full transparency into the IT asset lifecycle

Stage 4: In the managed stage, the managed organization is at the point where:

- Risks are measured and managed quantitatively and aggregated on an enterprise-wide basis
- Integration with other technology management tools (for example, Service Desk, Change Management)
- Performance metrics against functional requirements are monitored
- Process improvements are identified, implemented, and can identify breaks in processes.
- Full lifecycle management, cradle to grave, including all implications for contractual and financial management, and asset relationship with service level management
- Ability to identify long-term opportunities for standardization and cost recovery

Stage 5: Optimized state:

- Organization is focused on continuous improvement
- Process metrics are well-established, consistently analyzed, and process/service level performance is linked directly with IT management performance
- Fines and violations of software and hardware agreements do not or rarely occur
- Executive dashboard available to show trends (improvement and efficiency)

 Remember, periodic assessment functions as an aid in analyzing where you are against where you want to go. This determines your next steps that in turn define a practical roadmap for moving forward, using process development methodologies, and software tools.

Key initiatives that lay your foundation

Laying the foundation for a sound yet practical ITAM program means incorporating some guiding principles that help ensure a positive beginning. These principles apply not only to new initiatives, but also to project restarts that are common in most organizations. These principles are outlined as follows:

- **Be sure you obtain executive buy-in and support**: Everyone would love to have processes develop organically from the bottom up. However, the harsh reality is that, without buy-in from the executive level, process development becomes little more than functional or leads to departmental turf wars. Participation in the process development initiative must be a requirement, not an option.

- **Be sure to obtain peer support**: The idea behind ITAM and most other system management processes is to provide benefit to the organization as a whole. Ensuring peers receive this positive message is the best way to short circuit the kingdom building as previously mentioned.

- **Appoint an IT asset manager**: Someone must become the process champion, as well as assuming managerial responsibility for the tasks and functions associated with the process.

- **Create, approve, and implement a strategic ITAM plan**: The adage about failing to plan becoming a plan to fail is a truism. Live by it.

- **Develop, design, and disseminate your ITAM processes**: Be smart about your process, and realistic in what you want to achieve. Don't work alone, and don't keep others out. Mutually beneficial implementations should be shared.

- **Acquire or develop effective software for ITAM and discovery tools**: Use the best tools you can find and afford, even if that means developing them internally.

- **Implement an ongoing quality assurance program**: Be clear about your expectations for the ITAM process and monitor them to ensure those expectations are met.

ITAM fundamentals

Managing the **total cost of ownership** (**TCO**) while ensuring your organization's software and hardware are properly inventoried, updated and serviced. Maintaining a good balance of resources and control between centrally managed and network-distributed systems. Deciding how many of your information systems and how much of your systems management to outsource, if any. Ensuring the security of all your information, including everything transmitted via mobile devices. Choosing among proprietary, compatible, and open source software options to find the right balance of resource and control between centrally-managed and network-distributed systems.

These are just a few of the issues and challenges facing the CIOs and senior IT executives charged with IT management responsibilities. The proliferation of choices doesn't make the task any easier.

When developing any management process that works, there are certain principles and best practices that make up an effective ITAM strategy for your business. An effective solution must be supported by a robust end-to-end approach to ITAM transformation. The Activity Sphere Model, shown in the following screenshot, represents a best-practices approach, ensuring all critical tasks leading toward the development and implementation for an effective and efficient ITAM program are accurately scoped and securely implemented as planned.

Initial activities are undertaken with an eye to the total enterprise, ensuring clarity in each of the three key areas: vision, strategy, and policy. From there, focus intensifies on planning, designing, implementing, and maintaining the solution. The aim is always to support the processes, tools, and communication required in completing the ITAM transformation. The following illustrates the essential approach:

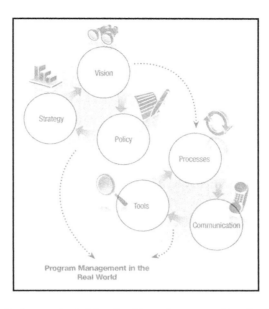

The McLachlan Activity Sphere Model leads directly to my **Tactical Framework Methodology**. This consists of five phases that ensure all aspects of the ITAM process that directly affect its success are addressed. The following illustrates the key drivers influencing this approach:

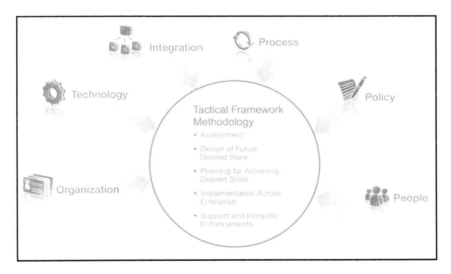

The **Assessment** step is the planning phase, where you will review the current strengths, weaknesses, and risks as compared to best practices and the requirements of your environment and business. All identified requirements are analyzed with a practical eye towards available resources and possible issues and concerns.

The assessment results should include gap analysis, strategic and tactical action choices, and recommendations. Deliverables from this step include:

- Measurement and reporting recommendations
- Improvement suggestions, prioritized by your needs and best practices
- A project charter that incorporates the findings of the assessments and includes the achievable goals, resources, benefits, and end results
- An outline of subsequent projects, including major milestones, broken into an estimated, reasonable schedule, based on information gathered

The **Design of Future Desired State** typically includes process redesign, where existing processes are adapted to include automation and standardization. During this step, the assessment results are refined into a roadmap. The roadmap should include: The expansion of processes with additional assets or locations, the development of new policy language, application of standards, implementation of automation, or the development of data to support tactical and strategic analysis. Depending on the assessment results and your choices, I always recommend creating the following planning tools to facilitate a common understanding:

- KPA-based action plan
- Data dictionary
- **Employee Awareness Plan** (EAP)
- Mapping of product capabilities to process requirements
- Systems review (data sources, complementary process automation)
- Updated systems architecture diagram
- Recommendations for standardized training

The **Planning for Achieving Desired State** step digs into the actions, resources, and time line required to implement the improvements that have been taking shape in the preceding steps.

The **Implementation Across Enterprise** step differs depending on whether a product implementation is part of the action steps. It includes delivery of the evaluation and recommendations, a project plan, specific tactical deliverables such as a data dictionary, and other specific deliverable as outlined later in the document.

For process-only projects, the implementation step typically includes process-reengineering, development of internal training materials, documenting the processes, and brokering cooperation between departments.

When a new solution is being incorporated into your environment, the implementation step includes installation of all products, loading of data, and the development of tailoring and customization to automate as planned for lifecycle management of the in-scope assets. Multiple product implementations may be conducted at the same time, which shortens the timeline and facilitates the development of a common understanding of the data elements and the reporting capabilities in both products.

Development during product implementation can include configuration, design and coding of the application, reports, notifications, workflows, and wizards. The time required for each of these items will depend on the complexity of the business rules that are being encoded. The vendor-supplied integration tools should be used to load the ITAM system or to integrate with other systems in your organization's environment.

The **Support and Integrate Enhancements** step reflects the inspirations that occur during the project implementation. These include new opportunities where unforeseen benefits are uncovered during the implementation. As success measured by goal achievement for the project becomes visible and enthusiasm for the project rises, and as employee awareness is conducted and grows, new requests for lifecycle management and reporting will arise. This is a good thing, and not something to be feared. Plans for these enhancements, as well as the training of internal staff and participation in the ongoing development and support of the process can be developed as part of a follow-on strategy.

This loose, tactical framework allows you to clearly articulate the steps and key deliverables required to enable the transformation ITAM brings to your organization. The activities shown in the McLachlan Activity Sphere Model are incorporated into this framework.

Solutions from full implementation of the entire asset lifecycle system to those addressing portions of an existing system that is either not functioning properly or missing some functions are available. Ongoing support for ITAM best practices and initiatives is required as the ITAM process matures. Regardless of the size of your implementation, both the Activity Sphere Model and the Tactical Framework Methodology help ensure the development of the very best solutions for your enterprise. Remember that ITAM is a *transformative* process, so change and adaptation are the norms.

Defining what ITAM is

There are many misconceptions within the business arena as to what constitutes an effective asset management strategy. For now, though, keep in mind that an effective ITAM process is a holistic discipline similar to the system management disciplines. It affects all aspects of the IT and resonates throughout the enterprise.

Before diving deeper into the ITAM process, let's look at what many companies do, believing they are implementing effective ITAM strategies. Look carefully to see if you can identify any of these in your organization.

What ITAM isn't

When developing your ITAM plan and strategy, the first step is to understand what is not ITAM. Many companies make the mistake of assuming they have an effective ITAM program in place because they possess one or more of the following:

- **Discovery tool**: this is not an ITAM Tool. Having the ability to discover physical assets is not the same as being able to manage those assets. While ITAM does include a discovery process, it also adds tracking of the physical, financial, contractual, and software information relating to that asset as it changes throughout its entire lifecycle.
- **Physical inventory repository**: While your physical inventory database may start out recording accurate data, the information is always changing due to IMACD (installs, moves, adds, changes, and disposals) within your organization. Additionally, physical inventories tend to be narrow in their focus, usually relying only on hardware and software configuration information.
- **Spreadsheets**: Far too many enterprises have users that rely solely on spreadsheets for recording their asset-related information. Typically, when spreadsheets are used to track assets, the focus is on getting some transparency into budgeting, as well as, users addressing the concerns of dissatisfied with existing technology or lack thereof. There tends to be very little standardization in the formatting and naming conventions used in the spreadsheets. In addition, the data is not continually updated and can result in multiple versions with varying data.
- **Fixed asset systems**: Its relative tax implications helps make the fixed asset system the favorite of financial professionals. However, it has little connection to either the day-to-day IT world or the costs involved with an asset.

A fixed asset system should never be used as a standalone system of record for ITAM, integrating it with your ITAM repository can yield reasonably accurate insights into the lifecycle of your equipment. It can also be effective in preparation for audits such as the **Sarbanes-Oxley (SOX)** compliance audits.

What ITAM is

For me, ITAM is the transformational program that cuts across organizations, lines of business and external sources. ITAM bridges the gap between operational and financial systems and processes, and provides critical information and knowledge required for your enterprise to make the best business and investment decisions possible, to ensure better contract negotiations, asset optimization, compliance, and accurate financial reporting. It can cover computer hardware and software, mobile devices, telecommunications systems, data, networks, and third-party contracts with consultants or hosted solution providers.

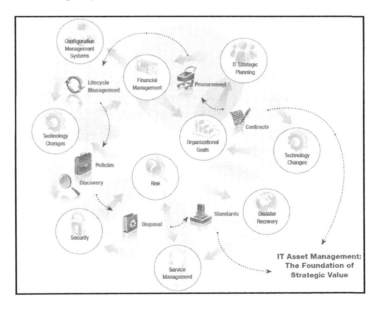

Framework of IT Asset Management

I believe and have seen with mid to large companies that I have worked with that fully supported and integrated IT and software asset management will:

- Reduce loss of software asset data and licenses

- Reduce risk of financial penalties due to non-compliance with licenses
- Reduce asset record gaps and duplications through a comprehensive central repository
- Reduce, eliminate and/or reallocate underutilized licenses
- Reduce, eliminate decentralize license compliance processes
- Improve productivity, efficiency, and quality through process automation
- Improve accuracy of software asset and license data and budget forecasting
- Improve understanding Total Cost of Ownership
- Improve accuracy of management reporting on software license positions
- Improve planning and execution with accurate hardware and software asset and license locations
- Improve staff understanding of policies and processes through compliance training

What objectives could ITAM cover or should cover for your organization? Think of pain points, areas of concern. Below are some examples of objectives for your ITAM/SAM program:

- Optimize utilization of IT assets over their entire lifecycle
- Provide accurate and consistent enterprise-wide asset information for planning and procurement, financial, accounting, consumption based pricing, application, and infrastructure operations, risk mitigation and reporting purposes
- Provide timely and accurate assessments of future asset needs to meet business and technology initiatives
- Increase visibility into the costs of procuring, installing, utilizing, and transferring IT assets
- Accurately assess and rapidly fulfill end-user software asset needs and requests
- Provide a foundation for a comprehensive IT Service Management strategy

Another tool I like to use and create is a responsibility matrix (RACI/RACSI). It helps everyone to understand who is accountable for specific areas and processes for ITAM and SAM. The RACI/RACSI describes the level of responsibility of various roles in completing tasks or deliverables that are needed for a project, process, or effort. No one team can do it alone. ITAM requires collaboration of various teams: software asset management, application owners, vendor management, procurement, hardware asset management (Infrastructure team), network, finance, human resources, and legal for success.

RACI/RACSI stands for:

- **R (Responsible)**: This is the person who does the work to complete the task.

- **A** (**Accountable**): This is the person responsible for overseeing that the task is complete and completed correctly.
- **C** (**Consulted**): This person may be used to weigh in on the task but is not necessarily responsible for doing the work on it.
- **S** (**Support**): This person is assigned to help the Responsible person. Like Consulted, but provides additional work.
- **I** (**Informed**): Persons who are neither responsible for doing the work, nor responsible for overseeing its completion, but who should be kept up-to-date on its progress.

Roles (R,A,C,I) / (R,A,S,C,I)

Activity	CIO	CTO	COO	HR	Users - Enterprisewide	InfoSec	ITAM Team	SAM Team	ARB	Application Owner	Business Owner	IT Owner	BUs (Non IT)	Infrastructure	Network	DBA Team	Change Management	Legal	VMO	CP	FP & A	VP of Finance	
Champions / Sponsors ITAM-SAM Program	I	A	I			R																	
Provides security and compliance policies and guidelines for ITAM-SAM	C	S, C		C	I	A	R										C						
Manages ITAM as E2E Process and coordinates ITAM business activities across groups						A, R	R	S, I	S, I			S, I		S, I			S, I	S, I	S, I				
ITAM-SAM Communications & Launch Plans	C, I		S	I		A, R																	
Provides financial guidelines for ITAM-SAM				I																R	A	C	
Forecasting Process				I																R	A	C	
Acquisition / Procurement Process							S, C, I	S, C	S	R				I	S, I	S, C, I	A	S					
Enforcement of Acquisition Process								S							R, S	A, R	R, S						
Entitlement and Software License Management Process																							
Validate Licenses, confirm license availability before assignment/deployment							S, C			A	R	R		I									
True Ups / Renewals / Upgrades							C, I	C	R	A, R						C	C	C, I	C, I	I			
SAM Audit Response Process	I	S, C					A, R	S	S					S	S	S	S, C	S	S, C	S, C			
Asset Deployment & Configuration Management Process						C, I	S, I		S					A, R	C								C, I
Network Management						C, I	S		S					A, R		I							
Disposal Process: Hardware and Software						C, I	S							A, R				I					
Disposal Process: Network						C, I								A, R					I				
Vendor Management Process		A					I	I	I								S, C	R	S, C, I				
ITAM-SAM Tool Admin: User Acct Administration							A, R																
Server Support for ITAM-SAM Tool: Infrastructure							I							A, R	S								
Supports ITAM-SAM Tool Database							I							S, I	S	A, R							

Sample responsibility matrix

One critical fact I want to point out is that both **hardware asset management (HAM)** and **software asset management (SAM)** are components of ITAM. You cannot do one without the other. So often, companies will want to implement a SAM program, but have no true hardware asset management. You can't do software asset management if you don't know where your assets are. Hardware asset management covers the management of the tangible aspect of hardware assets (for example: servers, laptops, desktops, mobile devices) and networks. HAM allows a company to:

- Track hardware and unused assets
- Identify theft or loss
- Manage inventory
- Reduce maintenance contract costs
- Carry out repairs under warranty

In order for IT asset management to be effective, the identification and tracking of key components must be performed frequently and regularly.

Working definitions for *ITAM* might look like this:

IT Asset management is the integration of the physical, financial, and contractual attributes of software and hardware used to provide cost-efficient, timely business services. As a holistic approach, it includes the management of the asset's identifiers, components, support and warranty details, costs, contract associations, and all events associated with the asset and its use within the organization. As a discipline, asset management enables the financial management of all IT assets, providing cost-effective stewardship of these assets as resources used in delivering IT services.

IT Asset Management means, a system of integrated management, processes, strategies and technologies that enables an enterprise to manage its assets throughout their lifecycle.

Tracking is *not* ITAM: Tracking vs Managing:

- Asset tracking deals with the physical characteristics of software in support of planning, deployment, operation, support, and service; installation/use data.
- Asset management deals with the fiscal (financial and/or contract) details of software as required for financial management, risk management, contract management, and vendor management; ownership data. *Asset tracking is a prerequisite.*

Implementing an effective ITAM strategy requires tools aligned to processes that are event-oriented and traceable. As with any vital process, intra-enterprise cultural and political shifts must occur at all levels. Simply put, accuracy in asset management, as well as the ability to develop a configuration management database, cannot exist without enterprise-wide and top-down support for the asset management discipline. Remember, the key question you are seeking to answer is this: Can we justify our IT spend without knowing the assets we have at our disposal? Without an effective asset management strategy, as well as the support this discipline requires, the answer is a resounding *No!*

ITAM is about more than simply storing asset-related information. Your strategy should extend to ensure the following capabilities:

- Deploying asset-related data
- Automating processes and procedures
- Understanding asset ownership and assignment
- Enabling efficient operations
- Reducing the risk of human error

Assignment - who physically possesses the asset?

This is distinctly different from ownership (financial burden) or accountability (who answers for asset integrity). Assignment tracks the actual possession and presumable use of the asset.

As obvious as this seems, many companies can't physically verify either the presence or use of many key assets. In conjunction with lifecycle status, assignment data gives the organization the information needed to physically account for critical assets and ensure effective use.

For active commodity assets, accountability and assignment may be assigned to the same person. For active service or network infrastructure assets, they will tend to be different. For inactive assets, accountability may be the asset team and assignment may be a store room. Having the data to physically locate an asset closes the loop on accountability and many regulatory requirements.

The goal to aim for is ensuring that all users requiring this information receive accurate data in a timely manner, and in a meaningful, standardized format. Once captured, asset-related information is useful for management reporting, financial reporting, audit preparation, and planning purposes. Information can then be linked between systems, using a single source of data, rather than duplicating the same information through multiple processes and storing it in multiple places.

The ITAM lifecycle

The IT asset management lifecycle covers the period from initial request for an item through procurement, delivery, stocking, deployment, monitoring, support, installation (as well as all moves, adds, or changes in location), upgrades, reuse, termination, disposal, and replacement. This lifecycle is sometimes referred to as cradle to the grave:

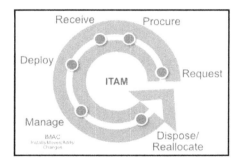

The ITAM lifecycle

Lifecycle status: this is the functional lifecycle a particular asset is at the moment, and if it's capable of providing its intended value. This is the foundational measurement for reconciling the asset's planned use versus actual use.

This is the most important and the most neglected asset data point. When you know the current lifecycle state of an asset at any moment in time, you can efficiently plan IT update/replacement, budget, **IMACD (Install, Move, Add, Change and Disposal)**, and procurement activities.

Six major components that form the IT Asset Management Lifecycle are as follows:

- **Identification of Asset Requirement**: The identification of the asset requirement component is the process of determining the IT asset needs of an organization and/or individual end-user. It is typically initiated by the user or the Business Asset Manager and requested via the Service Request Management process.

- **Planning**: The planning component is the process of determining if available IT asset(s) exist in inventory and/or identifying the IT asset purchasing requirement for a specific business unit or customer.
- **Procurement**: Once the planning component has been completed, and no IT assets have been identified as *available and in inventory*, the IT asset is ordered by following your organization's Purchase process.
- **Configuration and Deployment**: When the IT asset is received, the asset is verified and assigned both an Asset Management and Workstation/Server Configuration owner to configure, inventory, install, and deploy the asset in the environment.
- **Installs, Moves, Adds, and Changes (IMAC)**: Installs, Moves, Adds, and Changes are events that impact existing IT assets. In addition, major events such as new hire, and termination also impact the IT asset environment.
- **Decommission, Disposition and Disposal**: Technology refresh is the event that impacts both the disposition and disposal component of the Asset Management Lifecycle. IT assets are either leased or purchased depending upon the type of asset. Leased assets are typically returned to the Lessor upon reaching their lease expiration. Purchased assets may be retained in the environment if in good working condition or directly disposed of because they have reached the end of their useful life.

As an aid in understanding the basic ITAM principles and to better manage assets using established best practices, I have grouped the wide-ranging factors involved in this process into a simple, three-phase format, which I will go through in detail below. In facilitating this process, many mid to large companies appoint an asset manager, giving this key role direct access to the executive team. This access, and the resulting top-down support, is essential in implementing the guidelines required for an effective IT asset management program and system. It also helps ensure buy-in to the process throughout the enterprise.

Phase one – requests and procurement

This phase covers every action required to acquire an IT asset. This includes moving from the initial request and selection process through to asset delivery and training. Typically, the three processes involved in completing this stage are: request management, the approval process, and procurement.

Request management

The key elements are as follows:

- **Hardware requests**: Users submit their requests for IT equipment through a designated approval person or web-based request system. The request is then submitted and follows the approval workflows to enable control and accountability for spending and standards. At any stage of the approval process, the requester should be able to find out the status of the request. It is the best practice to limit equipment choices to a maximum of three for any type of equipment. This enables the support team to maintain a limited parts inventory on-site. It also allows them to focus their training and proficiency objectives on only three machines every year. It also lowers costs while decreasing the technical complexity of supporting a wide array of systems and peripherals. This also lowers demand for Help Desk support.

  When fulfilling hardware requests, all associated equipment required to make the equipment functional should also be included. For example, a request for a laptop would also include everything a user requires to make the laptop work for them: a monitor, a mouse, a keyboard, and docking station. Any standardized software packages required by the user's job function should also be included.

- **Software requests:** Software requirements should be included with the initial request. Software is often purchased at a discounted rate as part of the procurement arrangement with your vendor. Software is also sometimes loaded by that vendor prior to delivery or may be part of the requested standard image, based on the user's role. These standardized bundles also help control costs while improving supportability.

Another best practice is that a team, not an individual, handle procurement requests. If your organization is medium-sized or bigger, there will be many moves and changes coming in the course of a year. A team ensures coverage at all times.

The approvals process involves the following:

- **Budget**: Your budget must always be closely monitored. Fail in this and the results are serious consequences for approvers, and the organization. Costs change, as do support requirements. Ensure that the budget is always flush.

- **No delays**: The approval process itself is a frequent cause of delays in procuring required equipment. Again, if an individual is handling these requests instead of a team, expect delays. Life happens, as does work. Frequently, there are conflicts between the two. To avoid delays, have an automated process to forward the request for approval to another team member or to a more senior approver. Setting this contingency up within your procurement process will allow your organization to meet its **SLAs (service-level agreements)**. Even in a manual process, a copy of the request for approval can be sent up a level. It is critical that the procurement team monitors all requests and reports regularly on turnaround time. Departments or individuals causing too many delays should be reviewed, and solutions to the problems must be identified and implemented.
- **Stock:** A key component of any effective asset management process allows approvers to verify whether or not a requested item is available in-house, sometimes called reuse or re-harvest. This helps avoid unnecessary purchases. If requested equipment or software must be purchased or leased, health checks must be in place within the change management process to ensure all assets (hardware/software) on order are compatible with organizational policies. The change management process can also verify that incoming orders will not be affected by near-term strategic or organizational changes.
- **New hires**: It is essential that the acquisition process expedites equipping new hires. Standard new hire approvals must provide furniture and IT equipment essential to the employee's task. The **Human Resources (HR)** department should coordinate equipment assignments with procurement.
- **Denied**: When approval is denied, communication to both the requester and the procurement or finance team is essential. This must happen quickly.

Procurement process

For ITAM purposes, procurement is defined as follows:

The process defining how an organization obtains its assets. This includes receiving requests and approvals for goods and services (including standards, definitions, and vendor identification), and discounting targets and policies under negotiated discounts and contracts. The goal of procurement is to negotiate the best price for the best product and service meeting the organization's needs.

Other considerations within the procurement process include:

- **Key Suppliers / Strategic Partners**: Orders should always be placed with approved vendors. There are likely to be a number of approved vendors, usually one for each type of product. The service aspect will include the preferred arrangements for delivery and sometimes installation of the equipment.
- **Communication**: Inter-departmental communication is key in your ITAM program and process. The requested asset must be tracked throughout its lifecycle in your organization, from the time the order is placed until the asset is disposed of, either by obsolescence or other means. To aid in this communication, here are the roles of each process participant:
    - Finance expects to receive an invoice for the order and manage the payment of that invoice.
    - The asset manager anticipates delivery of all requested assets, and verifies verification that the equipment is logged sometime between delivery and release to the user.
    - IT technicians schedule installation, using a unique asset-tag identifier as part of the receiving process. This identifier, along with the asset's serial number, becomes the primary link between the asset and your asset systems. These identifiers must remain with this asset throughout its lifecycle. These identifiers should never be changed.
    - Training ensures that any hardware or software education requirements are scheduled and fulfilled.
    - Security or facilities management must be aware of the asset delivery, and upon arrival, verify that it meets the order's description and quantity. After verification, arrangements should be made to transport the equipment to the appropriate workplace.
- **Installation:** IT technicians install the equipment for the user, making sure that the equipment is fully configured and ready for use. The asset repository should be updated prior to deploying any equipment, and this should include all software installed. Best practice is to verify that the asset record matches the asset itself prior to it being entered into the CAR. This enables the asset to enter tracking with a clean and accurate record.
- **Deployment:** After delivery and installation, the user is given access to the network and all associated programs. Any additional training requirements should also be arranged at this time. To achieve best practice, user should always sign an acceptance form for the equipment after delivery and installation. This form should be kept in the employee's HR record, ensuring that the equipment can be retrieved if and when the individual leaves the organization.

- **Return of equipment**: Equipment delivered that either does not match the order or does not work properly should be returned to the supplier immediately. Entries should not be added to the asset repository, nor should the asset be paid for.

Phase two – change management

This phase explains the change management process involved in tracking an IT asset. Tracking is key because every time an asset is involved in a change, whether it be a move or a re-assignment, the organization incurs an associated cost. ITAM helps determine if these changes are handled in a manner that is cost effective, business effective or, in a perfect world, both. Factors to be considered during this phase include user management.

Change is the norm in most organizations. When changes occur, however, best practices require an organization to assert control over when and where changes take place. Workplace rules and restrictions are rarely compelling enough to ensure that every employee adheres to them. However, an unwillingness to control changes in the workplace often diverts key staff away from critical tasks and diverts funding away from key business development. The most common types of changes affecting assets are:

- Employee resignations/terminations
- Employee job changes
- Maintenance (beyond economical repair)
- Employee location changes
- Technology refresh
- Equipment getting lost, stolen, or damaged
- Equipment being re-deployed to another employee
- Operational or technology shifts

Any of these changes should initiate updates to the ITAM tool (**central asset repository (CAR)**). This should be done prior to releasing the asset for use. The asset manager monitors the overall process, and is ultimately responsible for ensuring the accuracy of the central asset repository.

Installs, moves, adds, changes, and disposals are important tasks in any business environment. Because of this, these types of changes should be completed under the control of the organization's change management ITAM processes. In fact, many forward-thinking enterprises develop an internal process for managing these types of changes.

This process is often referred to as **IMACD (Install, Move, Add or Change, Disposal)**. IMACD covers all day-to-day activities, including:

- Installation of hardware and software
- Changes to configuration
- De-installation and relocation of equipment
- Decommissioning of hardware and software

The objectives of these client services are to ensure that the aforementioned activities take place with a minimum disturbance of the business as usual operation. Activities concerning hardware relocation or de-installation, and changes to configurations, should be performed as scheduled and to the agreed standards, with minimum loss of end-users' productivity time. These objectives go hand-in-hand with the overall objectives of change management, so it makes sense that your IMACD process should be subordinate to your change management process. The goals of the IMACD process are:

- To enable control and accountability for updating a server or end-user environment
- To preplan as much as possible a change event or critical service or maintenance
- To reduce the amount of shadow support within the enterprise
- To build a database that helps define trends in maintenance and repairs as a feeder to the technical review process for creating catalogs of approved products

The best practice is to use these processes in determining any business benefits while demonstrating that the financial and resource costs are justified. Just be sure to include depreciation of equipment as a consideration, because equipment that is terminated within its planned lifespan often results in a higher cost.

Process accessibility

In order for ITAM to function effectively, it is crucial that all users follow established processes. To ensure compliance, these processes must be published and reviewed/updated at a minimum of once a year for the entire IT asset management lifecycle. Self-service solutions enable all employees to become familiar with the processes from their equipment. Staff members with clearly defined roles and responsibilities within these processes must sign off delineating their responsibilities when they take delivery of a new asset.

Record all changes in the CAR (ITAM repository)

All changes must be recorded in the CAR before assets are deployed. Users are over allocated, and the data-recording element most times takes a backseat to the role they are performing BAU (business as usual). The best way of facilitating changes to the CAR is to allocate responsibility for the change to the allocator. Role-based accountability is critical to the success of ITAM.

Policies and procedures

Your internal ITAM policies and procedures should make clear what changes are acceptable. It should also spell out the consequences for those who choose not to follow these processes. The core team, with full support from the key stakeholder, must clearly communicate ramifications. Your ITAM marketing communication plan (MARCOM) should focus on the value that ITAM will bring not only to the organization, but most importantly to the users as well.

Help Desk

The Help Desk, often known as the Service Desk, has an important role to play in the management of IT assets. Its primary role is to act as the point of contact for problem management, incident management, and service-level management. It can also act as an ongoing audit system for your ITAM process. Whenever the Help Desk receives a call, have the staff request the user's name and the asset number, crosschecking information within the Asset Management system with information shown on the screen.

Data accuracy

With ITAM, accurate data means knowing what equipment you have, where it is, how it's working, how much it's costing you, who's using it, what you can reuse, and whether it's doing for the business what you intended it to do. This knowledge plays an important role in how key people (stakeholders, peers, end users, and so on) perceive the success of you ITAM program.

Regular audits of both the CAR and the work locations are considered a best practice. While physical or spot audits help identify unused or discarded equipment, an automated inventory discovery tool helps locate equipment that has been moved or swapped, and has not been recorded in the asset repository.

Quality assurance

Health checks should be ongoing. Regular review of systems and procedures is essential, as are follow-on checks of the progress of suggested process improvements.

Phase three – asset disposition

The retirement of IT assets involves planning and managing the execution of retiring assets from the enterprise.

Planned obsolescence and asset retirement

Unused assets are difficult to track because they are usually not connected to the network. Enabling effective asset tracking and avoiding a surplus of assets requires that any increase in the asset stock should be accompanied by a corresponding decrease - either an exit or retirement - in older assets, linked to the new acquisition. Simply put, bringing new equipment into the organization should lead to older assets leaving the organization.

The process by which retired assets are disposed of must, in all cases, adhere to defined standards, procedures, and restrictions for the disposition/disposal of IT hardware and software in a legal, cost-effective manner, in accordance with federal, state, and local laws, including, but not limited to, regulating waste and respecting copyright and software licensing.

The core ITAM team, along with security and infrastructure teams should define the processes and methods for asset retirement and disposal. Common disposal events include:

- Obsolescence
- Lack of continued need
- Unable to upgrade required hardware or software
- Damage
- Excessive maintenance cost
- Replacement equipment or software received

Definitions

- **Disposition** refers to the reassignment, recycling, and/or disposal of IT equipment through responsible, ethical, and environmentally sound means.
- **Obsolete** refers to laptops/desktops and all other equipment which no longer meets requisite functionality and/or no longer under warranty.
- **Surplus** refers to hardware or software that has been replaced by upgraded equipment or is superfluous to existing requirements.
- **Beyond reasonable repair** refers to any and all equipment whose condition requires fixing or refurbishing that is likely to cost as much or more than total replacement.
- **Commercial Software** refers to purchased software, company is legally allowed to use. Unlike hardware, commercial software is not owned by the company. When purchased, a product's software license only gives a company the right to use the software, but does not transfer ownership rights to the company. Thus, the rules of use are mandated by the vendor via software licensing terms and conditions.

Allocating responsibility

Your process should include two levels of responsibility: overall responsibility for the function and responsibility for ensuring appropriate actions is taken. Each key action must be assigned to a staff member whose responsibilities are clearly defined. Responsibility for an action does not necessarily mean that the person given the responsibility actually carries out the action.

Acceptable methods for the disposition of IT assets are as follows:

- Used as a trade-in against cost of replacement item
- Re-tasked/reassigned to a less critical business operation function
- Recycled and/or refurbished to enable further use (within limits of reasonable repair)
- Disposed of through a certified disposal partner

It is the responsibility of your organization to ensure that IT assets are dispossessed according to one or more of the methods prescribed above. It is imperative that all dispositions are done appropriately, responsibly, and according to corporate IT lifecycle standards, as well as with company resource planning in mind.

The following rules must therefore be observed:

1. **Obsolete IT Assets:** As explained previously, *obsolete* refers to any and all computer or computer-related equipment that no longer meet requisite functionality. You should identify and classify when IT assets are obsolete. Decisions on this matter are sometimes made according to an organization's purchasing/procurement strategies. Equipment lifecycles should be determined by IT asset management best practices (such as total cost of ownership, required upgrades, etc.)

2. **Reassignment of Retired Assets:** determine reassignment of computer hardware to a less-critical role. Whenever possible - reassign IT assets in order to achieve full **return on investment** (**ROI**) from the equipment and to minimize hardware expenditures organization-wide.

3. **Cannibalization and Assets beyond Reasonable Repair:** Verify and classify any IT assets beyond reasonable repair. Equipment identified as such should be cannibalized for any spare and/or working parts that are worth the costs associated with removal. The IT department will inventory and stockpile these parts. Remaining parts and/or machines unfit for use can be sold to an approved scrap dealer or salvaging company after data wiping. Handling of any hazardous materials such as lead, mercury, bromine, and cadmium should not be done onsite, but should be contracted to a government-certified disposal company.

4. **Decommissioning of Hardware Assets:** All hardware slated for disposition by any means should be scanned to discover installed software and be flagged as decommissioned in the Central Asset Repository (which will release software to be harvested/reclaimed), before being fully wiped of all company data. Your IT department(s) should assume responsibility for decommissioning equipment by deleting all files, company-licensed programs, and applications, following your organizations *Information Security Policies & Standards.*

Hardware should be picked up by a reputable, environmentally certified recycling company in compliance with all local, state, and federal laws. The certified recycling company must provide credible documentation that verifies adequate data wiping, tag or label removal, and disposition and disposal that meet regulated environmental standards.

Some key points of regulations are:

1. All non-working/obsolete computer products should be disposed of in an environmentally sound manner
2. Monitors and terminals are always hazardous

3. Other components of a computer system (for example, circuit boards, keyboards, mice) could be hazardous depending on their lead, mercury, or cadmium content, which can vary from product to product

4. Substantial penalties may apply for non-compliance

5. **Decommissioning of Software Assets:** For old software that is no longer used, licensed or unused versions of commercial software, you must adhere to the terms and conditions of the governing license at the time of disposal, which will vary from vendor to vendor and from **operating system (OS)** to application software

Follow these guidelines to dispose of unused commercial software:

- Delete/Uninstall electronic media and software.
- Destroy the manuals.
- Keep all serial numbers, dates of purchase, dates of destruction, and means of destruction in the Central Asset Repository. This will provide a complete audit trail in the event of a software audit.

Other best practices related to asset retirement include:

- **Suitability for role**: Where possible, always ensure that training and qualifications of staff match the requirements of the task.
- **Training:** Each team member should be trained to accomplish the assigned task, and should have a clear understanding of how to carry out the assigned responsibility, as well as how his or her assigned responsibilities fit into the overall process.
- **Process and procedural documentation**: Employees should have open access to clear documentation outlining who, what, how, when, and why assigned actions are taken.
- **Return of equipment**: During the re-issue process for assets, either return equipment to stock or designate it for retirement. Equipment designated for retirement should be removed at the time of issuing the new equipment. An asset return form must be completed, with a copy sent to HR for inclusion in their records. This action can be automated with links from the asset management system to the HR system. Typically, an employee's manager assumes responsibility for the return of equipment, which can then be re-allocated to a new employee.

In situations and organizations where no ITAM system exists, you should be aware of the following potential issues or concerns:

- **Concerns for costs**: While the total cost of an asset can be difficult to calculate, the true cost of owning an asset is frequently the result of guesswork. Not having this information can be perilous for organizations because there is no clear means of defining which assets provide the best value as opposed to those providing little or no organizational value. Organizations working without ITAM fare poorly indecision making relating to asset procurement. This, in turn, results in spiraling costs.

- **Wasted resources**: Without a means to effectively deploy assets, the implementation of new processes can be problematic. Resources must be dedicated to identifying the location and ownership of missing assets, and to updating inaccurate databases.

- **Minimal order**: Believing that missing equipment may reappear, organizations are reluctant to write off missing equipment. This situation often develops as a response to other internal organizational pressures to acquire new equipment quickly, whenever required, without being concerned about removing old equipment.

- **Data Accuracy**: Accurate data must be maintained at all times. This applies to any items that are deemed to be assets of the company. IT assets often are the cause of heightened anxiety, because the equipment is often portable, costly and a possible security risk.

- **Business inefficiency**: Typically, organizations operating without the benefit of ITAM cannot answer these essential questions:
  - What assets do we own?
  - Where are these assets?
  - Who is using them?
  - What contract terms and conditions govern these assets?
  - Do we have the necessary software licenses?
  - What software is currently in use?
  - Are we adhering to the terms and conditions of the licenses?
  - What assets are still under warranty?
  - Are the guidelines for hardware and software upgrades being followed?
  - What are the total costs involved in the use of our assets?

Summary

In this chapter, you have learned if your organization is in a chaotic, reactive, proactive, managed, or optimized state when it comes to ITAM and what key initiatives you need to develop a sound foundation for your ITAM program. We have covered what ITAM is and isn't.

We have also covered the fundamentals and the lifecycle best practice for ITAM. The standard position of assets at a point in time doing the IMACD stages and where in the lifecycle process stage the asset is: control, procure, deploy, manage, or retire. You have also learned when planning ITAM:

- Don't *boil the ocean* by trying to manage too much at the beginning
- Don't create a central asset repository without reviewing how processes will keep the data complete and accurate
- Do leverage real business requirements to get there
- Do pull data from sources you know to be accurate
- Do pick the services that you want to manage
- Do ensure that processes are in place and reviewed

In Chapter 3, *The New Risk Management*, you will learn how to govern your ITAM program through policies, processes, and procedures. We will also provide, details on the various types of ITAM policies that you could have and what types of regulations and standards can affect your ITAM program, policies, processes, and procedures.

The New Risk Management 3

This chapter is all about governing your ITAM program through policies, processes, procedures as well as, details and examples on the various types of ITAM policies.

Policies, processes, and procedures

If we listened to and took to heart Colin Powell's declaration—*there are no secrets to success. It is the result of preparation, hard work, and learning from failure*, IT policies would be wildly successful.

Governing through policies, processes, and procedures

An effective ITAM program can be the difference between getting the most out of your assets and possibly leaking millions of dollars. Today's business world is moving at a rapid pace. Employees work longer hours, from more locations, and with more devices to get the job done. From mobile phones to laptops to iPads, the amount of number assets assigned to individual executives has grown considerably over the last 5 years.

Although ITAM has never been as cut and dry as counting how many desktops are in use and what software is installed (though it may have been that simple during the initial adoption of technology in the workforce many years ago), it has become more complicated and essential with moving assets on the rise and software vendors getting more complex with their software license models.

A successful ITAM and SAM program is essential for governing hardware assets, software assets, and mobile assets to minimize security risks, increase compliance, and manage costs.

It will be difficult for your organization to stay in compliance in the face of more frequent—and more expensive—vendor audits. The increasing mix of personal devices used for business also increases security risks and exposes your enterprise to substantial financial liabilities. The foundation of a successful ITAM program, with multiple moving assets, is a strict set of policies, processes, and procedures that are strictly enforced.

Tracking and consequences

Policies must address software and hardware acquisition standards, software asset management, and anti-piracy, software use, hardware and software decommission, software license harvesting and recycling, IT asset and inventory management, and the issue of missing or lost hardware and mobile assets, but rarely do they outline or enforce the penalties. Once employees are held accountable for a device, it's more likely they will take better care of the asset. Penalties include charging an employee for the value of the device or the threat of taking legal action against an employee if any action put the company out of legal or regulatory compliance.

Your organization also needs a uniform process to follow when theft or loss occurs. Your policy should address questions such as the following:

- *How long should the employee wait before reporting the theft or loss to IT?*
- *How long before the authorities are contacted?*
- *Can you erase the data on the mobile device remotely?*
- *Is the data backed up?*

Inaccuracies

When mobile assets are not part of the auditing process—as they are often forgotten or only a portion of mobile assets are audited due to poor tracking—an opportunity arises for unauthorized software downloads and use. Strict policy and procedures for software downloads and mobile apps need to be created and followed to prevent audit fines that could equal millions of dollars (especially, for a multinational company). A majority of companies don't know what is on their mobile assets, so they can't have an accurate inventory of software in their environment and do not know if employees are using the installed software. What is thought to be the usage amount is not always the case unless the company is constantly monitoring everything that happens on their mobile assets. Otherwise, they are out of compliance. I will cover software asset management and compliance in more detail in Chapter 4, *What is SAM?*

Data security

The very nature of mobile devices creates a corporate security issue. Users often work offline only to connect and synchronize information with enterprise backend systems once the employee is back at home (literally). Perhaps they are syncing e-mail or documents on an iPhone, Android, or laptop with their home computer. The risk is the lack of visibility the company has of each mobile device and where the information may be transferred.

With today's work habits, the blurred line between work and home can cause organizations to overlook possible security breaches that must be addressed by their ITAM and SAM policies that provide guidelines and standards on mobile, hardware, and software usage. On many devices, IT has the ability to pre-empt data security breaches with device controls or special configurations based on the device itself. In any case, you should have in your policies language that limit *what types of information can be sent using the mobile device, how it is used*, and *what happens should the device be stolen*. By keeping the most vulnerable information off a mobile device, you will minimize the risk from theft or loss.

Implementing a strict policy

No matter how strong your IT infrastructure/operations, if employees and assets are not properly managed, things can quickly get out of hand. Having a comprehensive set of policies in place, with a proper communication and education program for employees, will reduce problems during each phase of your ITAM program. Here are some tips for effective policy management:

Provide details: A good set of policies and procedures that specifically address mobile, hardware, and software assets will pre-empt any questions by giving employees comprehensive, well-thought-out answers. Questions or topics that can be covered in detail include:

- What are the policy procedures for my iPhone, Android, and laptop?
- Can I use my corporate phone for personal calls?
- Can I receive corporate documents to my phone through e-mail?
- How do I order a replacement security token for my laptop?
- Can I forward work e-mail messages to my personal phone?
- Can I take my laptop home?
- Can I use my corporate card to purchase software?
- Are there any restrictions to downloading and installing software on my laptop?
- What do I do if my mobile device is lost or stolen?

Get ahead of your users: Explain the most common scenarios and anticipate potential security threats before problems arise. Some industries, such as health-care or financial services, must follow stricter policies for compliance and privacy than, for example, a marketing agency that isn't subject to industry legislations.

You must also specify consequences for non-compliance. A strict policy is nothing if it is not followed.

Tips for implementing your policies

Once policies are in place, communication is key. It's hard enough to get employees to pay attention to something as significant as changing their health-care policy let alone to IT policies. Here are three simple steps to implementing policy:

1. **Presentation**: Many companies make the mistake of developing a 500 page manual and don't consider their audience. A young audience may prefer to watch a YouTube tutorial or participate in an interactive Q&A. Consider brainstorming for new and innovative ways to present your policy guide that will grab and hold your employee's attention. In high school drivers; education class, they always showed us a scared straight video of foolish young drivers becoming injured. Your ITAM/SAM education can stress the real-life and personal (not corporate) price to be paid for bad behavior with assets.

2. **Implementation**: Although we have seen the gigantic manuals employees must sign to verify they have read and understand the policy, the likelihood is that very few actually read it. Once again, think about your audience and how to make this fun and unforgettable for them. Perhaps a company off-site that incorporates fun activities and policy presentations or an interactive game every new employee must play to get up to speed.

3. **Ongoing education**: Without ongoing education, policies and procedures are useless as they can and will change, and as new employees are taken on. Ongoing initiatives reinforce the messages; they provide an opportunity to address new issues as they arise.

 Companies must adapt to their employee base—*what is going to get their attention?*

Don't let the process get you down

It seems simple enough to create and uphold policy, but 9 out of 10 times policies fail and nearly always the reason is due to a breakdown in the process. When the process stutters, it can systematically cause chaos and result in legal action.

Why the emphasis on process and the importance of policy? If any part of the process fails, it is highly likely that the policy has failed too and the organization is out of sync with one or more compliance rules. And, if the organization is out of compliance, it could mean millions in fines, or even jail time for the executives.

Policing policies can be a complex issue within an organization as there are many various policies, from HR to IT to communications. However, through well-defined procedures and well tested processes, maintenance and enforcement can be simple.

Differences between a policy, process, and a procedure are as follows:

- Policies address *what* you want to accomplish and *why* you want to accomplish it
- Processes address *what* takes place and *when* it takes place
- Procedures address *what* to do, *when* to do it, and *who* does it

 Scenario:

- **Policy**: Smile everyday, live longer!
- **Process (execution of policy)**: Read company joke of the day!
- **Procedure (enable the process that delivers action on the policy)**: I get into the office at 9:30 a.m., turn on my laptop, and open my e-mail.

By regularly reviewing your organizations policies against new or updated laws, landmark court decisions, and industry standards, you can not only determine where the liabilities are in your organization's policies and procedures, but you can also lean on professional associations to steer you in the right direction to ensure compliance.

Laws, regulations, and statutes that affect IT and software asset management will have a major effect on the content of policies.

Types of standards and regulations from organizations include, but are not limited to:

Standards and Regulations Organizations			
ISO – International Standards Organization	COBIT – Control Objectives for Information and related Technology	IAITAM – International Association of Information Technology Asset Managers	DCMA

PCT |
| EPA – Environmental Protection Agency

RIAA

Super DMCA

UCITA | NCCUSL

RCRA

Title 17

UETA | NEPA

ROHS

TRIPS

WCT | SOX

TLT

WIPO Performance and Phonogans Treaty |

This chapter addresses three primary ways of simplifying the process in order to optimize, control, and enforce the necessary policies, processes, and procedures:

- **Framework**: Separate policy, process and procedure for clarity, division of labor, flexibility and efficacy
- **10 issues to address before documentation**: Address these issues before starting the documentation process for creating more effective, enforceable risk management policies, procedures, and processes
- **Key documentation development process**: Planning, development, implementation, monitoring, and enforcement

But, first, we should address why policies commonly fail.

Why do policies fail?

No human system will ever be perfect, but it is especially, important that the risk management policies, processes, and procedures of your company come as close as possible, for obvious reasons! One security breach in a bank or investment house can literally be fatal in certain circumstances.

There are five primary reasons for failure of policies, usually due simply to a breakdown in the process:

1. **Lack of communication**: Make a vigilant, ongoing communication of existing and, especially, new or modified policies. Employees simply must be made aware not only of company policies and the attendant processes and procedures, but also of the consequences to the firm and the individual for failure to adhere to them. Awareness of the gravity involved needs to become part of the company's internal culture to succeed.

2. **Exceptions and inconsistencies**: Exceptions are continually made for every rule written. However, organizations need to guard against exceptions to the exceptions from creeping in without formal review and adoption. Exceptions no matter the circumstance or how senior the executive—can lead to inconsistent compliance with industry or government regulations and company policies. Vigilant monitoring is needed to guard against this, with clear lines of responsibility and accountability.

3. **Lack of clear responsibility**: If a company is not certain who is responsible for the implementation, monitoring, and enforcement of company policies, the reality is that nobody is accountable. This is a certain recipe for failure.

4. **Lack of ongoing training**: Companies cannot assume that all employees, especially new ones, have taken the time to read their employee handbook, where all company policies, processes, and procedures can be found. It is far more likely they have not. The solution is refresher training for the most important policies throughout the year, and onboarding procedures for new employees that include vital policy training.

   When changes to regulations such as PCI-DSS or SOX occur, it is critical that everyone involved be alerted and trained accordingly. If new internal procedures are needed, however small, to comply with processing credit card data based on PCI-DSS restrictions, make sure everyone involved in processing credit card information is notified, trained, and fully aware of the liabilities involved. If new categories are added or subtracted from the Fair Disclosure regulations under SEC regulations, it is critical that all senior managers be reminded that all market-making or significant company news be channeled through investor relations, and that exceptions or breaches will be dealt with swiftly.

5. **Lack of enforcement**: Once a clear hierarchy of penalties is established and communicated to employees, it is important to follow through with fair but swift action in the event of infractions. It is often not enough for people to know there are penalties involved for breaking the rules; all too often they require direct experience, too.

Framework

One of the most important means of improving the risk management function is to separate the three main components: policies, processes, and procedures. These terms are typically used interchangeably, and the resulting documents tend to become hopelessly over-engineered and confusing. Simply taking the time to understand the differences among these three categories, and separating them into discrete action items and documents, will go a long way towards streamlining the entire process.

What separates policy, process, and procedure?

They all address related subject matter, but at a different level and with different types of content. Each of them has a unique purpose that drives the content contained in each type of document.

Policy

Policies are the high-altitude business rules and guidelines that ensure consistency and compliance with the company's strategic direction. They articulate the business rules under which a company and all its departments should operate. Policies are the overall guidelines under which processes and procedures are developed.

Policies address *what* the rule is and its classification, *who* is responsible for the execution and enforcement of the policy, and *why* the policy is required. The relationship between a policy and the related processes and procedures is not one-to-one - policies are not part of the process/procedure, but processes/procedures must reflect the policies.

The common and key policies are as follows:

Common Policies	ITAM/ SAM	IT Security and Disaster Recovery	IT Administration	IT Software Development
○ Internet utilization ○ Download ○ Software ○ Anti-piracy ○ Anti-virus ○ Desktop utilization ○ PDA ○ Hardware ○ Acquisition ○ LAN/WAN ○ Security ○ Disposal management ○ Disaster recovery	○ IT asset inventory management ○ IT vendor selection ○ Hardware and software asset decommission ○ Software asset management and anti-piracy ○ Software and hardware acquisition ○ Software license harvesting and recycling ○ Mobile ○ BYOD	○ IT threat and risk assessment policy ○ IT security plan ○ IT media storage policy ○ IT disaster recovery policy ○ Computer malware policy ○ IT access control policy ○ IT security audits policy ○ IT incident handling	○ Information technology (IT) management policy ○ IT records management policy ○ IT document management policy ○ IT device naming conventions policy ○ TCP/IP implementation standards policy ○ Network infrastructure standards policy ○ Computer and Internet usage policy ○ E-mail policy ○ IT outsourcing policy ○ IT department satisfaction policy	○ IT project definition ○ IT project management policy ○ Systems analysis policy ○ Software design policy ○ Software programming ○ Software documentation policy ○ Software testing policy ○ Design changes during development ○ Software releases and updates ○ Software support policy ○ Software consulting services ○ Software training policy

Foundational ITAM/SAM policies you want to have in place at a minimum:

Hardware and Software Asset Disposition policy:

- This policy covers the disposal of IT Assets in an environmentally friendly manner according to state and federal law. Communicates and provides standards for data and software removal prior to disposition, and stipulates the organization's scope of obligation (if any) concerning donation and/or resell.

IT asset Inventory Management policy:

- This policy will establish and define standards by which your company will manage, collect, and report information about IT Assets under **Information Technology (IT)** control.

Software Asset Management and Anti-piracy policy:

- The Software Asset Management and Anti-piracy policy will educate the users on software types and the federal regulations covering copyright protected pieces. This policy will also outline the penalties for violation.

Example of the SAM Anti-piracy policy:

Policy:	Number:	ITAM 001
Software Asset Management and Anti-Piracy	Effective Date:	August 21, 20XX
	Supersedes:	New Policy
	Dated:	July 31, 20XX

It is important to manage software well, just as you would any other valuable company asset. Nahteava, Llc. and its subsidiaries and affiliates, (collectively "Nahteava") understands that all software is protected under copyright law and includes provisions granted by the software publisher as well as obligations stated in the End User Licensing Agreement (EULA). Nahteava is committed to complying with the requirements of the EULA and to preventing copyright infringement of all published works. Nahteava acknowledges that unauthorized duplication of software may subject users, officers, and Nahteava to both civil and criminal penalties under the United States of America Copyright Act.

1. **IT Asset Management**: Information Technology Asset Management (ITAM) is the process of tracking and analyzing the technical and financial information of an organization's hardware and software. This process spans the life cycle of hardware and software assets from the moment the asset is requisitioned through its procurement, receipt, deployment, maintenance and retirement. Nahteava will manage IT assets (hardware and software), working in conjunction with purchasing, vendor management, and the IT department. Software Asset Management will ensure Nahteava has a complete record of all software acquired for Nahteava IT equipment. Software Asset Management in conjunction with the Nahteava Legal Department will also be aware of the potential penalties for infringing copyright law.

2. **Software Piracy**: Software piracy is the illegal distribution and/or reproduction of software. Purchasing software is actually purchasing a license to use the software. That license spells out how you may legally use such software. Any time someone uses the software beyond the scope of the license, that person — or Nahteava — is violating the license agreement and copyright law. Whether software piracy is deliberate or not, it is still illegal and punishable by law. Software piracy can subject an individual to arrest and criminal prosecution, with fines of up to $250,000 and prison terms of up to five years. In civil cases, the software publisher can recover actual damages and the profits attributable to the infringement, or statutory damages of up to $150,000 per product.
    a. Types of Software Piracy
        i. **Corporate or end user:**
            1. Underreporting software installations acquired through volume purchase agreements
            2. Making additional copies of the software without having the proper number of licenses

       3. Swapping disks inside or outside of work

   ii. **Subscription licensing:**

       1. Using subscription-licensed software past the expiration date.

   iii. **Support Entitlement:**

       1. Accessing support entitlements (e.g., .DATs, super .DATs, updates, or upgrades) without a current agreement.

   iv. **Internet piracy:** This can occur in many different forms, including:

       1. Auction sites that offer counterfeit and/or outdated products
       2. Peer-to-peer networks that allow for unauthorized file sharing

   v. **Counterfeiting:** Someone attempts to copy the product and packaging to look like the original.

   vi. **Hard-disk loading:** Some unscrupulous suppliers illegally install software to help sell computers. While many suppliers are authorized to install products onto the machines they sell, honest vendors supply the software via agreements with software vendors.

3. **Duplication:** Nahteava will not duplicate media or documentation unless expressly authorized to do so by the software publisher. Duplication of software will only occur for archival and disaster recovery purposes, with ownership of this process residing in the IT department and oversight by the IT Asset Management Office, Software Asset Management (SAM).

4. **Education:** All Users will have access to software policies to ensure full understanding of processes, as well as consequences, for not adhering to anti-piracy policies.

5. **Software Acquisition:** Software will not be acquired through user corporate credit cards, office supply, petty cash, or personal expense budgets. All software will be purchased through appropriate Central Procurement and/or Vendor Management contact with approval and validation provided by the Software Asset Management team. Acquisition channels will be restricted to ensure proper registration, inventory, and support information is recorded.

   Software Asset Management (SAM) monitors when new and prohibited software is installed on Nahteava systems. Purchases made outside of the acceptable processes will not be reimbursed and will be removed from company computers. *Reference the ITAM Software and Hardware Acquisition Policy.* [Insert policy link]

6. **Software Disposal:** *Reference the Hardware and Software Asset Disposition Policy. [Insert policy link]*

7. **Software Management:** Software will be registered in the name of Nahteava and not individual users. An inventory of software licenses will be maintained, updated regularly and compared to inventory of installed software. Software Asset Management (SAM) initiated internal audits will be conducted. Software license inventory will document the

title and publisher of the software, date and source of acquisition, location of installation, and serial number of software. Media, documentation, and serial numbers will be stored securely, with access only available to designated installers. Whenever possible, licenses will be harvested from retired machines and redeployed, rather than purchasing new licenses.

8. **Shareware/Freeware:** Shareware and freeware are copyrighted works with EULAs. It is Nahteava policy to follow and adhere to EULA requirements and acquire and register products in the same manner as commercial software products. Shareware authors will be paid the fee they specify for use of their products.

9. **Open Source Software**: Open Source software must be managed in the same manner as commercial software: the organization must understand licensing requirements and be aware of any changes to these agreements, such as commercialization of such products. These products may be covered under General Public License (GPL), GNU Library or "Lesser" General Public License (LGPL), or MIT License (MIT). Support contracts may be purchased and will be managed in the same manner as other support contracts.

10. **Home Use Rights:** Company-owned software may not be taken home and installed on employee owned computers, unless permission is granted through a licensing agreement where the publisher has granted home use licenses as part of the contract. Nahteava commits to tracking any licenses installed for home use and monitoring use of media and software serial numbers to ensure only approved installations are completed.

    Personal owned software may not be installed on Company-owned computer(s) and/or Company issued mobile devices. Users must understand licensing requirements and be aware that uses of non-commercial software for commercial purposes are prohibited.

11. **Storage of Media, Proof of License and Serial Numbers**: All media and serial numbers will remain securely stored; with access granted only to staff that require them for software installation and distribution. Serial numbers will not be shared with any staff not authorized to complete installations. Proof of license will be filed in a secure location and will be accessible to Software Asset Management.

12. **Mergers and Acquisitions:** Any companies acquired or merged with Nahteava will be required to provide an IT asset list to calculate the value of the IT assets. This inventory will include, but is not limited to, a hardware and software inventory of desktop computers, laptops, servers, mainframes, network devices such as routers and switches, and communication devices.

13. **Divestitures:** Before finalizing details of a divestiture, suppliers must be contacted to determine which licenses, if any, can transfer with the divestiture, and what the process is for completing the transfer. Where applicable, written notification on letterhead detailing the name of the buyer, number of licenses being transferred, product name and version,

and serial numbers will be sent to the publisher within 15 days of the divesture being finalized. In cases where suppliers do not allow their licenses to transfer, notification will be sent to the divestiture organization to inform that the product cannot be transferred and will need to be purchased from the publisher. In addition, notification will be forwarded to the publisher, to inform that the product will no longer be in use.

Be sure to note if there are any additional fees, and document the entire transfer process closely (this documentation is important because the company needs to be able to prove compliancy in case of an audit). If additional fees are excessive, investigate options to migrate to alternative products, including a cost/benefit assessment to calculate feasibility. Update the documentation regularly.

14. **Compliance/Non-Compliance:** Adherence to this Policy is the responsibility of all users (, and is mandatory. All users have a duty to report any known or suspected violations of this Policy to the Nahteava IT Asset Management Office (ITAM), Information Security (InfoSec), and/or the Legal Department immediately so that prompt remedial action may be taken. Investigation of alleged violations of this Policy will be the responsibility of ITAM, InfoSec, and/or Human Resources.

"**Users**" means all Nahteava employees (whether full-time, part-time, intern, per diem, independent contractor or temporary), service providers, vendors, contractors, consultants and other third parties given access to Nahteava 's IT assets (hardware and software).

15. **Coordination, Administration, and Revisions of the Policy; ITAM Program Administrator:** The individual in charge of overseeing this Policy as of the date of its creation is the IT Asset Management Program Head, (hereinafter, the "ITAM Program Administrator"). Users should direct any questions or report any issues regarding the Policy to the ITAM Program Administrator.

The ITAM Program Administrator is responsible for: (1) overseeing, monitoring, managing, maintaining and coordinating the implementation of, training for, and compliance with this Policy on a periodic basis; (2) assessing existing risks to Nahteava; (3) developing ways to manage and control such risks; (4) monitoring third-party vendor arrangements to ensure software compliance; and (5) testing and revising this Policy in light of relevant changes in technology and threats to Policy information. The ITAM Program Administrator will seek the guidance and assistance of IT, Legal, Human Resources, Vendor Management, Central Procurement, Internal Audit, and Information Security as necessary. Any new policies or procedures with respect to IT Asset Management and Software Asset Management must be approved by the ITAM Program Administrator and the Nahteava Chief Technology Officer.

Only the ITAM Program Administrator and Nahteava Legal have authority to revise this policy, although variances may be approved. This policy will be reassessed on an annual basis and revised as appropriate.

Software and Hardware Acquisition policy:

- This policy will standardize the acquisition process throughout your company allowing the organization to maintain control over the acquisition of software and hardware, and installation process of software.

Software License Harvesting and Recycling policy:

- This policy will establish and define standards, procedures, and restrictions for software license harvesting and recycling of software in accordance with copyright and software license agreements. License re-harvesting and recycling both involve reclaiming and reallocating unused software licenses.

Example of SAM License Harvesting and Recycling policy:

Policy:		Number:	ITAM 004
Software License Harvesting & Recycling		Effective Date:	August 21, 20XX
		Supersedes:	New Policy
		Dated:	July 31, 20XX

The purpose of this policy is to establish and define standards, guidelines, and restrictions for software license harvesting and recycling of software in accordance with copyright and software license agreements. License re-harvesting and recycling both involve reclaiming and reallocating unused software licenses.

1. **Software Management**: Software will be registered in the name of Nahteava and not individual users. An inventory of software licenses will be maintained, updated regularly and compared to inventory of installed software. Software Asset Management (SAM) initiated internal audits will be conducted. Software license inventory will document the title and publisher of the software, date and source of acquisition, location of installation, and serial number of software. Whenever possible, licenses will be harvested from retired machines and redeployed, rather than purchasing new licenses. *Reference the Software Asset Management and Anti-Piracy Policy.* [Insert policy link]

2. **Software License Harvesting:** License harvesting involves identifying machines with licenses not currently being used or being under-utilized. For example, licenses not being used by certain end-users or business units within Nahteava, and/or computers in storage that contain installed software. Where this situation exists, Nahteava can recover these licenses in order to avoid new software spend and/or potentially reduce annual maintenance costs. When re-harvesting "unused" apps, application metering is used to track usage and find candidates for re-harvesting. Exceptions are made for users with annual, seasonal or periodical.

3. **Software License Recycling:** License recycling is the process of reclaiming licenses from retired hardware. At configuration management, all equipment must be checked for software installed prior to data erasure, on all major operating systems. *Reference the Hardware and Software Asset Disposition Policy.* [Insert policy link]

4. **Check End User License Agreements (EULA):** Vendors may have certain restrictions on how often software licenses can be recycled. When engaging in license re-harvesting and recycling, it is important to know what the vendor agreements stipulate, otherwise Nahteava could become non-compliant. *Reference the Software Asset Management and Anti-Piracy Policy.* [Insert policy link]

5. **Retirement/Re-harvesting Guidelines**:   The Central Asset Repository will ensure that software and related assets are tracked and flagged as removed, recycled and/or reused where appropriate and in compliance with information management requirements. The Central Asset Repository will support the processes to ensure that:
    a. Deployed copies of software are removed from retired hardware (where it is permitted for licenses to be removed).
    b. Licenses and hardware assets which can be redeployed are identified for redeployment.
    c. Assets transferred (re-harvested) to other parties, and are transferred taking into account any confidentiality, licensing or other contractual requirements. For example, in the case of divestitures.
    d. Licenses and hardware assets that cannot be redeployed are properly disposed of.
    e. Records are updated to reflect the changes above, and audit trails are maintained of all changes.

6. **Coordination, Administration, and Revisions of the Policy; ITAM Program Administrator:** The individual in charge of overseeing this Policy as of the date of its creation is the IT Asset Management Program Head, (hereinafter, the "ITAM Program Administrator"). Users should direct any questions or report any issues regarding the Policy to the ITAM Program Administrator.

   The ITAM Program Administrator is responsible for: (1) overseeing, monitoring, managing, maintaining and coordinating the implementation of, training for, and compliance with this Policy on a periodic basis; (2) assessing existing risks to Nahteava; (3) developing ways to manage and control such risks; (4) monitoring third-party vendor arrangements to ensure software compliance; and (5) testing and revising this Policy in light of relevant changes in technology and threats to Policy information. The ITAM Program Administrator will seek the guidance and assistance of IT, Legal, Human Resources, Vendor Management, Central Procurement, Internal Audit, and Information Security as necessary. Any new policies or procedures with respect to IT Asset Management and Software Asset Management must be approved by the ITAM Program Administrator and the Nahteava Chief Technology Officer.

   Only the ITAM Program Administrator and Nahteava Legal have authority to revise this policy, although variances maybe approved. This policy will be reassessed on an annual basis and revised as appropriate.

DEFINITIONS:

"Nahteava" collectively means Nahteava, LLC. and its subsidiaries and affiliates and/or the business unit for which you are doing work.

"Central Asset Repository" is an IT Asset Management tool/system that allows control and management of all IT assets throughout their lifecycle from one location. Information maintained is as follows, but not limited to end-user, location, software installed, software license, hardware details, purchase amount, contract, and maintenance/warranty details.

"IT Asset Management (ITAM) Office" means the Nahteava organization responsible for providing the processes, tools, and support for managing Nahteava software and hardware entitlements and asset inventory.

"Users" means Nahteava employees (whether full-time, part-time, intern, per diem, independent contractor or temporary), service providers, vendors, contractors, consultants and other third parties given access to Nahteava 's IT assets (hardware and software).

Process

Processes are related activities that produce a specific service or product (examples, acquisition to deployment, procurement to payment). The majority of processes cross departments or functional areas. Each process designates the connection points and where it crosses department lines. The documentation presents the total process. It is helpful to be able to reference or drill down to the applicable policy or procedure for a process step. A process map is a useful tool to graphically display the process.

Processes indicate where there is a separation of responsibilities and control points. They are also very helpful to identify policy and procedure requirements. Processes address *who* is responsible for performing the process (department, division), *what* major functions are performed, and *when* the function is triggered.

Best practice models that can be used as a guide to create ITAM processes include:

- IAITAM/IBPL
- ISO
- COBIT
- CMMi
- Six Sigma
- PMI

The unique toolkit I designed addressed all areas of the ITAM KPAs.

The following figure illustrates the typical use of these models utilizing the **McLachlan Lessons Learned Best Practice** (**MLLPB**).

This is a workshop-based model that identifies where the money is, both for cost reduction and improving controls:

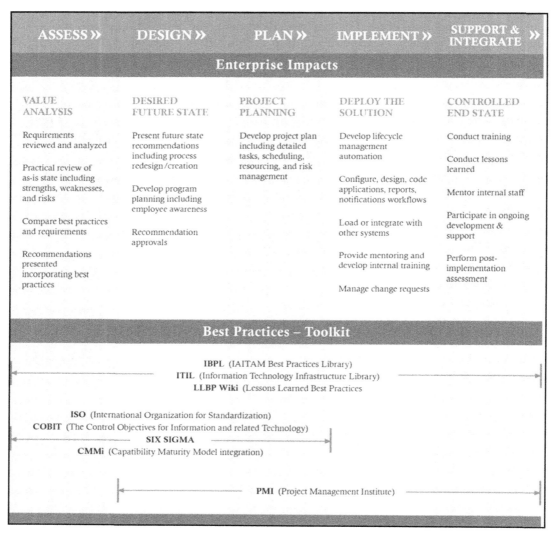

As discussed in Chapter 2, *ITAM Strategy and Plan* you should always conduct an assessment and gap analysis to evaluate and understand your organization's current environment (policy, process, procedure, and systems), explore the desired state, and conclude with an informative gap analysis.

This reveals the full scope of opportunities for savings, projected costs, and schedule, design requirements, and boundaries for your ITAM and SAM program. To determine the maturity level and state of an organization, I conduct what I call a **Heat Map Diagnostics** health check.

Heat map diagnostics – key process areas

A heat map is a simple graphic representation of the condition of processes and procedures within an organization. It captures the strengths and weaknesses of an organization's current ITAM practice, against industry best practices in the twelve **Key Process Areas** (**KPAs**). The results are defined against various Industry models and are represented using the ITAM process framework. Other models that were consulted include CMMi, Six Sigma, and ITIL. The ITAM process framework defines twelve KPAs, within each KPA there are specific practices that define the attributes of the process.

The example of the following heat map highlights areas of special concern and accomplishment:

Acquisition	Asset ID	Communication & Education	Compliance	Disposal	Documentation	Financial	Legislation	Policy	Program	Project	Vendor
Defining IT Asset Acquisition Process	Define Receiving Process	Communication Process	Define Audit Process	Disposal Record Requirement Process	Define Archive Process	Define Invoice Reconciliation Process	Define Legislative and Regulatory Advocacy	Define Policy Requirements	Defining Standards for Technology	Define project validity review process	Define Scorecard Process
Defining Negotiation Process including T & C	Define Acceptance Process	Education Process	Define Compliance Requirements	Prepare Asset Removal Requirement/Process	Define Archive Requirement	Define Budget Standards	Define Legislative and Regulatory Requirements	Define Policy Review Process	Define project estimating process	Vendor Crisis Management Process	
Defining the Request Process	Define RMA Process	Change Management Process	Define Process Review	Disposal Requirements	Define Documentation criteria Requirements	Define Chargeback Process	Define Legislative and Regulatory Tracking Process	Define Policy implementation process	Define ROI Requirements	Define project performance review process	Define vendor rules of engagement process
Defining Approval Process	Physical Inventory Process	Define Training Content Requirements	Define Process Implementation	Define Software Harvest Process	Define Documentation review process	Define Service Costing Process	Define Legislative and Regulatory Action Plan	Define Policy Effectiveness metrics	Define Program Projects	Define project benefits and cost process	Define vendor consolidation process
Defining the Redeployment Process	Define Asset ID Tagging Process	Define Communication Content Requirement	Define Audit Swat Team Process	Define Disposal Security Process	Define project documentation Requirements	Define Contract Review Process			Define Program Scope	Define project business case process	Define vendor gifts and gratuities guidelines
Defining the Asset Selection Process	Define asset ID tagging change control process	Define Vendor Communication Policy		Disposal Process *include remote	Define Collection and Input of Historical data	Define reconciliation with Fixed Asset Process			Baseline	Define project change process	Define Criteria for vendors classified as strategic
Identify Suppliers	Determine under reconciliation Process	Define Policy Communications Process		Define Disposal Due Diligence Process ** Advisor	Define Documentation Workflow Strategy	Define cost metrics and review process			Cost Benefit Analysis	Define post project review process	Define vendor business offerings
Prepare Justification Process	Determine Rejection Criteria			Define Storage Process					Business Plan	Define project risk management process	Define Vendor information update
Prepare Request Process	Determine Rejection Process			Define reconciliation process					Process Automation	Define project QA process	
Prepare Asset requirements				Define disposal audit process					Risk Management	Define post implementation resource reallocation process	
Identify Key Suppliers									Define program roadmap	Define project closure process	
Prepare RFI/RFP/IFB Process									Define MoU requirements	Define project resource selection process	
Prepare Lease Process									Define Integration requirements		
									Define Reporting strategies for all KPA's		

Heat map

The color-coding of each box represents the current condition for each project. Specifically, the color-coding used is defined as follows:

- **Green** indicates the practice is satisfied because clear, solid evidence was found clearly documented, widely known, understood and practiced, processes are accurate and repeatable, and recommendations for improvement may/ or may not be not required.
- **Amber** indicates the practice is partially satisfied because some evidence was found however, some processes were inaccurate or non-repeatable, and recommendations are provided.
- **Red** indicates the practice is not satisfied because no or little evidence was found or not performed consistently, however, few (if any) processes were accurate or repeatable, and recommendations are provided
- **Gray** indicates the practice area is not assessed and a health rating could not be determined for lack of supporting information

Every enterprises heat map looks different. I have some organizations that are all red when they first begin, and some that are mature in their program with half KPAs green. However, on occasion they are downgraded to yellow, because the process is not communicated well and users circumvent the process, without them realizing it.

IT asset management function model

I also like to create an IT asset management business function model that represents the processes associated with each lifecycle phase. Here is an example; each white box represents an individual process that qualifies for further detailed process flow diagrams:

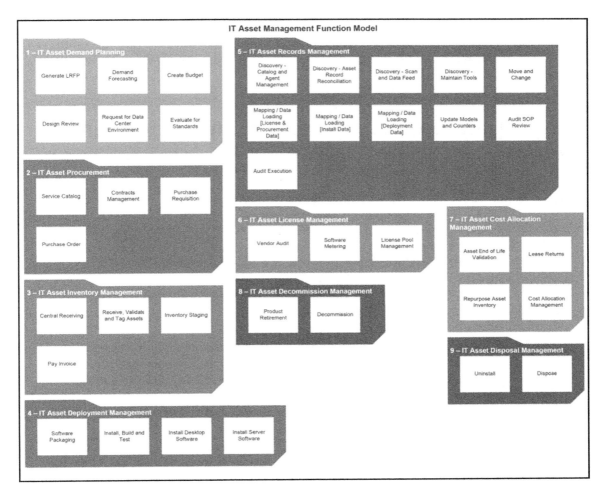

IT asset management function model

The preceding function model is just one example. There are various ways to illustrate.

Procedure

Procedures are the street-level steps necessary to perform a task or part of a process. They can take the form of a work instruction, a desktop procedure, a quick reference guide, or a more detailed procedure. They are usually structured by subject (for example, system instructions, report instructions, or process tasks).

A procedure usually addresses only a single task. This separation enables procedure components to be compiled into special procedure manuals for specific audiences and purposes. Procedures detail *what* steps are necessary, *when* the steps should be performed, and *how* they should be performed.

Why separate policy, process, and procedure?

There are at least four compelling reasons for creating a framework that separates the three P's and allocates the work to the appropriate level of the company:

1. **It simplifies things**: Policy is generally thought of as the domain of senior management. For regulated standards as prescriptive as PCI-DSS, as complex as SOX, or as aggressively enforced as U.S. copyright law, title 17, and the **WIPO Copyright Treaty** (**WCT**), a policy document can be as brief as two or three pages. Removing the complexities of process and procedure from policy documents simplifies the recurrent policy review process required by PCI-DSS, SOX, title 17, and many other regulations. And since risk management policies generally consist of elements required to achieve compliance, there usually is not much to debate.

2. **It allocates responsibility efficiently**: With senior management focused on overall policy, individual departments are free to focus on the minutia of defining procedures that fulfill the policy, and department chiefs can focus on the cross-functional processes. This division of labor will improve comprehension and buy-in enormously. Instead of responding to a three-inch policy binder from senior management where their relevant requirements are buried in Appendix IX, the lending department or the claims adjustors can respond to a three-page policy document by contributing aligned procedures and processes for the areas they know best. The final result may still be a 350-page manual, but it will be the work of many and well understood by all.

3. **It speeds implementation and promotes efficiency**: The problem of procedures and processes that are out of alignment with company policy are much less likely to occur when each level of management helps author the appropriate processes and procedures, based on company policy. Detailed procedures and processes are also much more likely to make sense from a daily implementation perspective when they are authored by the people directly involved, who understand what will stimulate or stymie appropriate behavior.

4. **It facilitates flexibility**: The division of labor reflected in separating policy, process, and procedure also helps to facilitate changes in policy, process, and procedure when necessary. Simplified two-three page policy documents for individual categories such as PCI-DSS, SOX, and copyright law are easily reviewed and modified when the regulated requirements change. Lower echelons of management can then make the necessary adjustments to cross-functional processes and task-oriented procedures, as needed.

10 Issues to address before the documentation process

Once policy, process and procedure are separated, there are at least 10 issues which are discussed as follows your company should keep in mind before, during, and after the documentation process that articulates the policies the company will follow:

1. **Define the purpose and content of the documents**: The purpose of every policy, process, and procedural document is extremely important because it defines the potential audiences and end users, the learning required and the work environment, and level of detail required. Be sure the different types of policies, processes, and procedures are carefully identified in advance of articulating them to prevent redundancy and to create a more complete roadmap.

2. **Targeted audiences**: One size does not fit all when it comes to documentation audiences. Understanding audience needs and wants, how and what they use for search criteria, and what they consider critical to their personal success should guide and inform the way documentation is structured and written. This type of understanding will affect the formats and styles used for documentation, and highlight the inconsistencies between audiences on terminology.

3. **Process flow**: Preparation of a cross-functional risk management process map is essential at the start of any documentation process. It is important to understand whether processes cross departments (for example, acquisition to deployment, procure to pay) in order to fully understand the context of document content. This helps establish the scope of a process, as well as the critical inputs, outputs, and control points.

4. **Predefined templates**: Consistent formats for different types of documentation not only make it easier for authors to create documentation, it also makes it easier to convert them to a content management system. Predefined formats make content categories consistent so that users know the type of information contained in a document, furthering the goal that documentation be intuitive.

5. **Documentation tools**: Never assume that documentation developers know the tools they are using. If the documentation developers are from their respective areas of expertise, they may not be familiar with the authoring tools, best practices, interview techniques, and so on, needed to develop effective documentation. Multiple authors can be a major source of inconsistency between documents. You should either train the authors on how to use the tools or hire experts, who can develop the documentation better and more efficiently.

6. **Consistent terminology**: Consistent terminology among all documents not only enables easier document access and use, it also allows documents to be categorized and moved much more easily to a content management system. Documents that use multiple terms for the same thing can cause great confusion for users; consistent terms are the cornerstone for classification development.

7. **Review and approval system**: Different types of content require different people or teams with the appropriate expertise to review and approve it. If content requires statutory controls (for example, SOX), appropriate professionals need to review it for the specific requirements. Documentation that is missing or misinterpreting key information will not fulfill the company's policy requirements. Complex subjects and processes may benefit from a walk-through during the documentation process to address and resolve potential issues.

8. **Testing and verification system**: Policy, process, and procedure documentation must be tested to verify that what is written is precisely correct. Testing should be performed with the user in mind, ideally as a walk-through of each step the documentation addresses. Although this is time-consuming, there is no other way to verify that documentation is 100% correct. Failure to test and verify could cause serious problems in terms of compliance and wasted time.

9. **Version controls**: Documentation must be controlled to ensure that correct versions are used. If there is no content management system, the documentation still must be controlled for future updates and access. Version control does not necessarily mean that all documentation is located in a central repository, but, at a minimum, the authors should know who controls it. Version control prevents redundancy and loss of valuable knowledge.

10. **Implementation, distribution and training plans**: The best time to plan for implementation, distribution, and training of new or updated processes and procedures is before the documentation process. Often left to the last minute, poor implementation and training are among the primary reasons for policy failures in companies/enterprises. Ideally, all users should be trained on the new processes in order to ensure they are understood. Part of implementation and training is change management, which enables the user to notify the company of errors, omissions, and recommendations.

Key documentation development process

Developing the documentation that codifies policies, processes, and procedures is itself a roadmap process that requires thorough planning and expert management. The documentation process should yield what everyone involved wants—risk management policies, processes, and procedures that are easy to access, easy to understand, easy to follow, and easy to explain. The information should be concise, complete, up-to-date, and correctly aligned with appropriate regulations, and the procedures and processes should be as intuitive as possible.

There are four phases involved in the development of policy, process, and procedural documentation:

1. **Planning**: Including strategy, guidelines and teams
2. **Active development**: Including investigation, articulation, and verification
3. **Implementation**: Including communication and training
4. **Monitoring and enforcement**

Phase one – planning

As the old saying goes, success in any endeavor requires planning your work before working your plan. This is especially true for developing risk management policies, processes, and procedures in the financial services industry, considering the level of regulation and the sensitivity of the data involved.

Strategy is always the first step, where appropriate managers gather to:

- Define the subject of the policy, process or procedure (which have been separated into separate document processes, ideally)
- Describe the purpose and scope of the policy, process, or procedure
- Identify the affected parties and end-users
- Map out any cross-functional territories the policy, process, or procedure may affect
- Ensure the resulting policy, process, or procedure conforms to overall company strategy

Guidelines are the established standards related to developing uniform, consistent documentation, including:

- Templates to guide authors as to data categories, length, and focus for each type of document—policy, process, procedure.
- Tools to be employed (content management, SAM, and so on).
- Nomenclature to ensure consistency of terminology among all documents, facilitate searches, and comprehension.
- Version controls regardless of the technology used, version control is vital to ensure that authors and users have the correct version of a document, including updates and other changes.
- Teams for each documentation task are assigned once strategy and guidelines are established. Ideally, team members should represent the appropriate knowledge required for the specific document (for example, purchasing managers for purchasing processes and procedures) and the level of management (for example, senior management for most policies, middle managers for cross-functional processes, and so on).

Phase two – active development

Once the preliminaries are completed, the actual work of developing policy, process and procedure documents flows logically.

Investigation comprises of:

- Interviews with end users to determine priorities, land mines, and practical realities
- Careful study of pertinent regulations to ensure company compliance and document alignment with the appropriate laws
- Preparation of appropriate process flows to determine areas affected by the policy, process, or procedure
- Determination of system functions and document structure

Articulation comprises of:

- Compilation and analysis of data collected during investigation
- Classification and prioritization of content, including exceptions to the rules
- Drafting and team review/revision of the policy, process, or procedure

Verification by the team comprises of:

- Hands-on walk-through exercises of the process or procedure to ascertain practicality, ease-of-use, and understanding
- Adjustments to correct any inefficiencies, errors, or missing information
- Final submission to legal and/or senior management for final review and approval

Phase three – implementation

Any time significant new policies, processes, or procedures are being introduced into an organization; it is absolutely essential to implement them properly. Most people are resistant to change and learning new ways of doing anything, and failure to implement properly can be a costly mistake. The keys to effective implementation of new policies, processes, and procedures include:

- **Communication**: Before, during, and after implementation. Let people know that changes are in store and why they are important to the company, and every individual within the company. Reinforce those messages during implementation with dashboards, e-mail updates, department meetings, town hall style meetings, whatever it takes to gain buy-in, understanding, and cooperation.
- **Training**: This includes of all affected personnel as needed to ensure they understand the new policies, processes, or procedures, and how to perform their work within the new rules.

Phase four – monitoring and enforcement

No matter how thorough the planning, development, and implementation, or how easy the processes and procedures might be new policies, processes, and procedures are virtually meaningless without ongoing monitoring and enforcement of the rules.

- **Ongoing monitoring**: This includes monitoring of the new policies, processes, and procedures is not only critical to ensure employee conformity with the new rules, it is often required for company compliance with regulations and laws. It's a good idea for you to keep a step ahead by self-monitoring and making adjustments and corrections, as necessary.
- **Enforcement**: This is the final step in the policy/process/procedure documentation process. In certain cases, such as deliberate fraud, enforcement is a matter of the law, which means turning the situation over to the appropriate regulatory body, the police, and the courts. For less serious transgressions, such as failure to adhere to every step of the procedures for acquiring software, it is up to each company to determine the level of punishment. In both cases, it is important that employees be fully aware of the consequences of not complying with established, well-communicated risk management policies, processes, and procedures. Above all, you need to make it clear who is responsible for enforcing company policies, processes, and procedures, so that there is no question where that responsibility lies.

Summary

When people have enough information to justify forced rules from jaywalking to corporate policies, there are some measures that can be taken to ensure that ITAM and SAM policies/processes/procedures do not fail.

Policies should be:

- **Clear and precise**: Policies should be easily understood with precise *if/then* directives. If there are regulatory reasons for the policy, those reasons should be included as a justification for the said policy. Additionally, if technical support or help desk service may be needed, instructions including who to contact should be easily found.
- **Easily accessed**: Similar to employee benefits, policies should be retrieved without difficulty.

- **Unambiguous about punitive actions**: Looking at industry regulations, laws that govern society, and other legal policies, there are always distinct punishments for non-compliance. IT policies should have the same clear-cut reprimand. Without it, IT policies mean little.

Organizations must:

- **Review**: Like any industry regulation, it's a good idea to review your IT policy annually as environmental changes—such as new technology, regulations, and business adjustments may affect them.
- **Communicate**: One of the biggest reasons why IT policies fail is that organizations do not effectively communicate new or existing policies well nor is there a program that helps to continue to reinforce policy changes.
- **Enforce**: Once a policy is broken and the punitive actions are clear, if an organization fails to take action, the policy becomes moot.
- **Present a united front**: From the highest executive to middle management, it's important to have everyone on the same page as to the importance of policies. Too often, managers also break the IT policies very publicly. Similar to parenting, executives and managers need to be on the same page by saying and doing the same thing.

Both awareness and willingness to comply as well as the other proactive factors listed are what your organization should take to determine the ITAM/SAM policies, processes, and procedures effectiveness. However, it is important to remember that compliance does not and should not determine the effectiveness of the policy in achieving its goals as it may not accomplish the desired outcome.

Examples of this—compliance becomes so costly that it causes more damage or prohibitively adds to IT costs than remedies the issues such that the costs of compliance are so great that it takes up millions to implement and manage, while giving little back year-over-year. For example, while an ITAM/SAM tool may initially reveal some startling cost savings, you have to consider that against the overall investment (short and long-term). For instance, *how difficult is the installation and implementation? Does it require specially-trained consultants? Will these ongoing consultants be involved in an ongoing manner due to the complexity of the enterprise and the software? What's the cost structure as a handful of ITAM/SAM tools are modeled after the dreaded annual maintenance cost structure?*

Compliance may be possible, but does not adequately achieve the desired objective. If the intended goal is to create a strategic ITAM program that addresses the needs of the enterprise from strategy to tactical, but only the discovery process is implemented, showing some initial cost savings results, the mandate remains unfulfilled. The underlying problem to be solved was not understood well enough to identify the right solution. Therefore, the policy and process put into effect is not effective. In this case, the policy and/or process would only address a small portion of the tactical ITAM program and very likely leave off vital elements including contract management, disposal, security, regulatory issues, communication, and education.

While it is seemingly easier to identify, plan and create IT and software policies and processes, organizations need to take more care with the procedures, communications, and enforcement efforts as well as accountability of its objectives. Think about how many times you've downloaded free software apps, made or accepted personal phone calls on your company's mobile phone, or even sent out or received personal e-mails. It's likely that one or more of these actions are not acceptable based on your corporate IT policy. Now, ask yourself *what you would do if you were responsible for the maintenance and enforcement of the IT policy?*

The next chapter goes over another key component for ITAM success, SAM. The chapter will cover what SAM is, the various types of SAM standards, how to manage software assets, and understanding software agreements/contracts, and license types.

4
What is SAM?

It's hard to explain why **Software asset management (SAM)** is so laborious, tough, onerous, burdensome, demanding, difficult and why it requires so much effort and why it takes so long to get perfect results. One, it will never be perfect. It's on going, constant change, which is why it must be actively managed, controlled, supported, and communicated within your enterprise. SAM is not just having a list of software discovered in your enterprise or comparing purchased licenses with installed software. Once, you realize that, you start to understand the complexity which we will cover in this chapter.

Software, license, contracts, money pit

SAM is the business practice of managing and optimizing enterprise software within an organization. SAM provides the governance framework that covers the request, purchase, deployment, maintenance, use, harvesting, and disposal of software. Why should anyone including the CEO or CFO care about SAM? Three words: money, efficiency, security.

Software takes up 20-35% of the typical IT budget and enterprise software purchasing and upgrades are on the rise. With enterprise application software alone, Gartner research forecasts a worldwide growth to more than $201 billion in 2019. With organizations typically over- or under-license by approximately 30%, an effective SAM program could mean significant savings in the first year and a continual 10 to 15% reduction in the **total cost of ownership (TCO)** year-after-year. This could mean millions in savings in the first 5 years.

Software licensing is increasingly complex. Even as vendors promise to work on simplifying their licensing models, the sheer enormity of managing software licensing can be overwhelming. In all likelihood, your organization has and works with several software vendors, which intensifies and complicates the entire process. At the heart of any SAM program is the ability to truly understand and interpret a software vendor's contract(s) - specifically the *terms & conditions* and the licensing models and changes.

The first and foremost fact that any organization should understand is that purchasing software from a software vendor does not mean you own the software. It means you are purchasing the *rights* to use the software within a certain set of conditions - as stated in the contract.

A successfully implemented SAM program will result in:

- Reduced audit exposure and financial risk to the enterprise
- Reduced security risk from unauthorized software within the environment
- Minimized cybersecurity risk
- Improved budgeting process and financial controls
- Increased operational efficiency

As part of ITAM, SAM encompasses the infrastructure and processes necessary to effectively manage, control, and track software assets through all stages of their lifecycle. SAM plays a significant part in this, with software accounting for an ever-increasing percentage of overall IT budgets. Successful SAM programs reduce a variety of enterprise risks, improve the budgeting process and financial controls, increase operational efficiency and save significant amounts of money every month, and every year if proactively managed and supported.

According to industry analysts such as Gartner, the average company is over-licensed on around 30% of their inventory and typically at least 30% under-licensed in other areas. And while this may sound nicely balanced, rest assured the software vendors and licensing watchdogs won't agree! Every year, organizations waste millions in purchasing additional licenses that they didn't need - whether it be because they fail to re-deploy existing applications, don't take advantage of bulk/enterprise licenses, or fail to go through the proper procurement channels.

Successful Implementation of SAM programs

Everyone talks about the benefits of SAM, but it's rare that we actually hear about quantifiable results. There are plenty of reasons for this including a lack of standard measurement, incomplete strategy, poor planning or execution, or the lack of tools to measure results. There are plenty of reasons but having a real return on investment with measurable results will show executives and give them reason to understand and support SAM as an ongoing initiative.

The C-suite didn't buy it

I hear this one a lot. But the fact is, no C-suite worth its salt would say no to a program that delivers so key benefits. If you can't sell your C-suite on the necessity of a SAM program, you either didn't do your homework sufficiently, or didn't zero in on the benefits that would get their attention. What would get the undivided attention of senior management? Let's review some points here:

- First year savings of up to 45% and ongoing annual savings of 15-30%
- 98% risk reduction from non-compliance with regulations such as SOX and PCI-DSS.
- 98% risk reduction from software licensing non-compliance, which could cost thousands of dollars, or millions, depending on the size of your enterprise.
- Operational efficiencies that help the organization become more competitive, profitable, productive, customer-focused and prepared for growth.

Let's address some of the benefits of a successful SAM program with some real results:

Reduced audit exposure and potential financial risk to the enterprise

With a **proactive and dynamic** SAM program, you are 98% prepared to face an audit and answer any questions the vendor may have. SAM is the insurance and assurance needed to ensure that you and the enterprise won't come up short on licenses or any other *little* issue.

Case and point: in 2010, a Fortune 500 financial services company was being audited by Adobe. The initial cost of license true-up was US$3.6 million, which would have blown away the remaining annual software budget set aside for much-needed HR and payroll software upgrades and enhancements. Through a comprehensive SAM best practices methodology and our organization's proprietary predictive analytics, the potential $3.6 million vendor audit fine was negotiated down by more than 75% to a little more than $800,000. In the case of the financial services company being audited by Adobe, three SAM areas were optimized to reduce spending:

- Leverage enterprise agreements
- License optimization (no more and no fewer licenses owned than required to meet contractual obligations)
- Reduced maintenance expenses

Reduced security risk from unauthorized software within the environment

With SAM tracking usage, users, how, when, where, and what is being used, it increases security assurance and reduces or eliminates unauthorized usage and prevents the resulting damage that can occur. User and IT service management reduces work inefficiencies by 50% when unauthorized software access and downloads are eliminated. The limitation of unauthorized or even illegal access to software proactively prevents security gaps. By limiting access, software deployment can be easily tracked and identified. The savings in operations and support costs taking a significant downturn allows the organization to focus on more important business goals.

Minimized cyber security risk (SAM + IT Security)

SAM has data IT Security can leverage around software installations, versions & editions, ownership, location, entitlements, assets & CIs. IT Security has standards and data that SAM can incorporate in their process on software black lists, software white lists, and user last login.

By working together and collaborating, these two groups will be able to protect your organizations infrastructure from security threats.

Having all this data intelligence will allow your organization to respond rapidly to identified security vulnerabilities. Software that have ceased to receive product updates and security patches from vendors. SAM will enable your company to quickly discover how many devices and applications are in the environment, along with their location, if they are under maintenance/support that are vulnerable. This information allows IT to proactively carry out more timely security patches and identify security threats sooner.

A holistic ITAM and SAM program will enable your organization to address the following key cybersecurity initiatives:

- Securely manage software assets and promote cybersecurity best practices
- Provide full transparency of IT assets across the enterprise to ensure a secure IT infrastructure that provides an effective defense against cyber attacks
- Protect the organization from data loss, employee downtime, and negative reputation resulting from data breaches

Case and point: What you want to avoid; in 2017, a credit reporting agency had a massive data security breach that could have been prevented, by applying a patch. Attackers entered its system through a web-application vulnerability that had a patch available two months prior to the breach. 143 million people's personal and financial data was exposed, and not to mention the bad press for the company; calling into question the organization's competence as a data steward.

This all could have been avoided if the security team had leveraged the information from the ITAM/SAM team proactively. They would have been able to receive a report that listed installed software assets in their IT environment and monitored for vulnerabilities. For this case looking for the Apache Struts 2 open source component used in one of their applications. They would have been able to quickly, and correctly mitigate and remediate the finding.

Improved budgeting process and financial controls

As much work as SAM programs may take during the strategic planning and implementation process, the fact is that this enables any organization to control its IT finance function down to the penny. A successful inventory of your software assets combined with the usage information will help you budget for future growth, M&A activity, and give you better control of software purchases.

An energy services provider that supplies over 600,000 residents in the Midwest with natural gas and electric wished to assess its current asset management practices and develop a more effective means of tracking them. During the discovery process, insufficient and inadequate policies and procedures were uncovered; where policies did exist, they were not being followed by employees. The company also needed stronger discovery and reconciliation processes. In order to rebuild the client's ITAM strategy, significant modifications were made, including integration of SAM information with financial and contractual information. Additional technology to support the lifecycle asset management program was acquired and put into action. The company's software acquisition and implementation processes were modified to include a central repository and to ensure ongoing compliance with software licenses. The Midwest energy services provider saved over $2.2 million by decreasing procurement of non-essential IT assets including software licenses.

Increased operational efficiency

While SAM programs are often housed under the IT organization, it is or should be a cross-functional program that takes into account all areas of the enterprise. SAM is fundamental to IT and to operations. When your software is running at its optimal level, employees have what they need in terms of licenses, and usage is being properly managed to alleviate unauthorized use. The organization as a whole will benefit from increased operational efficiency. Also, as part of its policies and practices, SAM programs create increased operational efficiencies across the enterprise in a multitude of areas including:

- Standardization of the IT environment
- Identity management
- Purchasing and distribution of software
- Procurement process
- Resource distribution or re-distribution

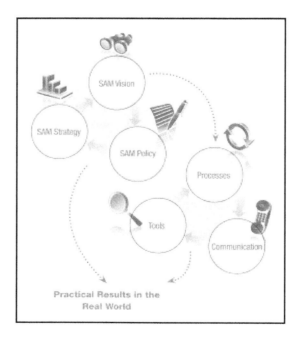

Alphabet Soup - ITIL, ISO

Whenever SAM comes up, we hear a lot about concepts, methodologies, standards, best practices, and the like. Certain acronyms crop-up time and again - especially ITAM, ITIL, and ISO. The fact is, this could get extremely confusing, and the descriptions of each sound similar, or even the same, with much overlap. While there is some overlap among them, they each have an important purpose. Whether an enterprise adopts one or more of these standards, it is always wise to know something about them.

What is ITIL?

Information Technology Infrastructure Library (ITIL), is a set of concepts and practices for IT service management, IT development, and IT operations. ITIL provides descriptions of IT practices and comprehensive checklists for implementing certain IT activities, such as SAM. ITIL/SAM is the entire infrastructure and processes necessary for the effective management, control, and protection of the software assets within an organization, through all stages of their lifecycle.

One such practice that ITIL outlines in detail is SAM. Under the definition of ITIL, SAM is the *practice of integrating people, processes and technology to allow software licenses and usage to be systematically tracked, evaluated and managed. The goal of SAM is to reduce IT expenditures, human resources overhead and risks inherent in owning and managing software assets. SAM represents the software component in IT asset management.*

What is ISO 19770?

The International Standards Organization (ISO) launched ISO/IEC 19770 an international standard of processes and procedures for effective software asset management. Designed to help manage risk, meet corporate IT governance requirements, and generally improve the cost-effectiveness and availability of business software across the enterprise, the standard's process includes:

- **ISO/IEC 19770-1** provides standards for an integrated set of SAM processes and procedures, divided into tiers for incremental implementation, assessment and achieve immediate benefits.

- **ISO/IEC 19770-1** (revised 2017) changed from a SAM standard to an IT asset management standard, focused on governance and alignment to other ISO standards (that is, ISO/IEC 55000, ISO/IEC 27000, etc.); covers lifecycle management requirements and addresses concepts such as BYOD, outsourcing, and cloud computing.
- **ISO /IEC 19770-2** provides specifications for creating **software identification tags (SWID)**. The tags are XML files installed alongside software and used for discovering and identifying software to optimize its identification and management.
- **ISO /IEC 19770-3** provides software entitlement standards focused on capturing and defining the information necessary to describe how software may be used to better enable companies to understand the assets they've already purchased.
- **ISO/IEC 19770-4** provides specifications for an information structure to contain Resource Utilization Measurement information to facilitate ITAM.
- **ISO/IEC 19770-5** provides an overview of ITAM and SAM principles and approaches, as well as, consistent terms and definitions.

My stance on the various frameworks, industry standards and best practices for ITAM, SAM, licensing, audits and so forth are that they are guidelines, reference points, steps to help you begin and progress. Every organization, enterprise is different. What works for one, will not always work for another. You take the standards, frameworks, best practices and adapt those standards to what works for your organization.

How Software Asset Management reduces risk and exposure

Not having a properly implemented or ongoing SAM program can lead to issues in all aspects of your organization, from financial management to **Sarbanes-Oxley (SOX)** compliance issues to security threats. These inherent issues lead to major risk exposures throughout the enterprise.

Some examples of potential issues and risk that can exist:

	Issues	Risks
Financial management	Incomplete and/or inaccurate corporate financial reports due to absence of data on: deployed and entitled software, financial commitments in software contract terms and conditions	Unable to: • Meet financial goals • Prepare accurate corporate financial reports • Prepare financial management reports (that is, forecasts, budget to actual expenses, chargeback calculations) • Provide financial management and control over planned and active projects involving software
Asset management	Inaccurate or incomplete reconciliation of data in IT asset management system and financial systems	Inadequate management of software assets due to: • Missing, incomplete and/or inadequate audit trails and systems interfaces between the software asset management system and the financial system • Inadequate and error-prone manual or automated reconciliation processes
Security	Inadequate tracking, monitoring, and control of software downloads from both authorized internal portals and unauthorized external sources. Inability to monitor for potential software vulnerabilities.	Lack of control over what software is introduced and used to meet business functions: • **Download from internal portal**: inability to track and control software for purposes of license compliance, chargeback, change control, maintenance • **Download from external sources**: potential introduction of nonstandard/unsupported software, as well as software with malicious code, and violation of license agreements Software vulnerabilities can lead to major security breaches.

SAM lifecycle	Absence of a linkage between a specific piece of software on a specific server/host or workstation to its associated asset record, purchase order, and vendor contract Inability to track and manage software throughout its lifecycle, starting with acquisition to deployment to disposal (No repeatable processes or standards.)	Potentially inaccurate and incomplete data regarding the disposition and location of software assets leading to: • Inability to create an accurate Central Repository (ITAM) / Configuration Management Database (CMDB) or to rely on the accuracy of the existing ITAM/CMDB • Adverse impact on effective management of key IT functions, including software refresh, software reuse, patch management, and so on. • Inability to maintain accurate inventory of available software may result in purchasing unnecessary software • Inability to harvest or reuse software licenses
Contract Management	Inadequate or missing processes to capture software contract terms and conditions in a standard manner to facilitate compliance self-assessments Software and hardware contracts not shared with ITAM or SAM teams; visible only to strategic sourcing or vendor management or procurement	• Manual processes to reconcile contract terms with actual practices may be error prone leading to legal and financial consequences • Barrier to standard contract language and business rules to facilitate contract negotiations, as well as subsequent compliance • Inability to easily determine the impact of changes to terms and conditions or product pricing Inadequate management of software licenses due to: • Missing, incomplete and/or inadequate contract details, terms and conditions, systems interfaces between the software asset management system and the contract system • Inadequate and error-prone manual or automated reconciliation processes • Delayed response to software audits

Software Usage	Absence of complete and accurate usage data about deployed software	Potential payment for under-utilized or unused software • Financial or legal exposure due to compliance with usage metrics • Inaccurate chargeback for software usage Missed opportunities to identify alternative and/or cheaper alternatives for software products having limited use
Order and Fulfillment	Inadequate standards and controls around the process to order, approve, and fulfill requests for software	• Inability to acquire and deploy software in an effective and efficient manner to meet business needs • Introduction of products that do not meet business, functional or technical requirements • Lack of or inadequately controlled authorization process and spending limits for software

SAM programs can be complicated but will make your life a whole lot easier and less risk for your organization if willing to take the time to understand and implement SAM correctly and fully. With the benefits that I've outlined, there is still a vital part of any software asset management program and that is *how*. Once the benefits derived from the SAM program are made clear, these guidelines will help you to begin thinking about the process and implementation of your SAM program.

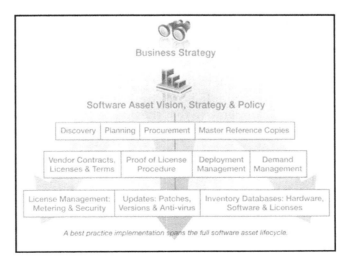

Four steps for managing your software assets

The steps for managing software assets are as follows:

Step 1 - D is for Discover

In any comprehensive SAM program, the first step is a robust discovery or internal audit period. Discovery should include a list of all active, inactive, stored, and remote hardware (PCs, laptops, servers, repositories, and backup systems) and the software products. In addition to searching and capturing your assets, you must also collect all copies of proofs of purchase. Sometimes this even means the shrink wrap, as these will have codes on them to validate your purchase. During this time, gather original copies of media, certificates of authenticity, and proofs of purchase (current RFPs, POs, invoices, and receipts).

This is where you assess what you have, who has it, how it's being used, proof of ownership, and lastly, but most importantly, how it matches with your contract Terms & Conditions.

While there are many tools out there that can be leveraged for an initial asset management discovery period, it is critical to note that not all SAM tools are created equal and can be a costly investment. Ideally, there needs to be a physical audit to validate an automated output from an asset management tool, if one exists. Often, the validity of a discovery tool is in question; thus, a complete physical audit that validates the accuracy of the discovery tool is beneficial. Otherwise, offer the physical audit a more reliable solution than the discovery tool, which can be subject to errors.

Reconcile your IT and Legal

As part of the initial discovery process, it should be common practice to reconcile your software asset with the legal documents - from proof of ownership to the actual governing Terms & Conditions. While many think to reunite proof of ownership with each software asset, reconciling software licenses with the current governing software vendor contract happens much more rarely. It is imperative that the license is reconciled with the governing SLA in order to be in compliance and avoid issues should a software vendor audit arise.

Software reconciliation is achieved by determining the purchase position - by contract and by installation position per product. Contracts provide use rights/restrictions (i.e. geographical coverage). Purchases are based on purchase data contract designation or associated to contracts based on least restrictive usage rights by product. For example, if a product has multiple contracts, the global level contract provides the most flexibility in product usage over the regional or country-based contracts.

Step 2 - I is for inventory and C for central repository

A central repository could be an advanced inventory system, or even an excel sheet (not a good choice for mid-sized to large corporations, government agencies, or universities), whichever works best. The purpose of a central repository is ongoing, proactive, dynamic management and maintenance. Whenever a new piece of software or user changes or enters your organization, it must be recorded in the repository. Maintaining an inventory of all software licensed to your organization in the central asset repository (ITAM/SAM tool) with automated discovery makes it much easier to provide proof of ownership for a complete list of assets in your organization's environment. The automated discovery system ensures the updating of inventory data when new software enters the system. It also allows you to secure the original and backup copies of proof of ownership documentation and installation media.

Regularly scheduled full (annually) and spot (quarterly) audits ensure that data integrity remains high. Regular audits of the system also verify accuracy and eliminate illegal software. Updating both the onsite and disaster recovery repository after each audit ensures the backup data remains current. As changes occur with your organization, they must be reflected within your repository. Otherwise, you may end up with improperly assigned or used assets. Very often, the organization will end up paying for assets that aren't being used.

Step 3 - L is for lifecycle management: from procurement, deployment, and tracking to ongoing management

Often overlooked, lifecycle management is an essential part of a successful SAM program. From procurement to retirement, every asset should be inventoried and evaluated to be sure the asset is delivering the value needed.

A lifecycle status tells us where in its functional lifecycle a particular asset is at the moment, and whether it's capable of providing its intended value. This is the foundation datum for reconciling the asset's planned use versus actual use. Oddly, this is both the most important and the most neglected asset data point. If you know the current lifecycle state of an asset at any moment in time, you can intelligently plan, the IT update/replacement, budget, **IMAC** (**install, move, add, change**), and procurement activities. For example, if you know that an asset is available but not assigned, you can manage internal stores and plan inventory levels—or identify key assets that are not providing direct value.

If you know an asset is ordered but not received, you may need to track a shipment status. If you know that an asset is retired, you can begin physical recovery, software harvesting, and disposal activities.

Procurement

One of the three main issues with SAM stems from the procurement process. With annual maintenance and support costs for the first year at 20% of the total software purchase price (not to mention the built-in increase), within 5 years of the initial software purchase, you'll have paid more than 200% for your enterprise software. Creating a centralized procurement office or committee is essential to controlling costs and managing your software assets - similar to how a household or a business would view and manage their finances. Unfortunately, there are three main challenges with procurement to the enterprise:

- **Siloed groups**: Whether by department, region, or country, many large organizations have different purchasing policies and procedures. Often, as with any IT purchase, software licensing purchases overlap and lead to over- or under-licensing.
- **Buying simply for discount**: The procurement or purchasing agent may not necessarily be the user or the IT decision maker. It may very well be an administrator or internal finance executive. The issue of not understanding the organization's or group's IT or operational needs intimately will likely lead to higher expenditures on software in the long term since the purchase will probably be based on the pricing discount versus the actual short- and long-term needs of the group.
- **Lack of policy and procedure**: A major concern with any process, but especially the initial procurement of software, is the lack of a policy or procedure. In many organizations, software is often procured on an *"as needed"* basis, meaning that as the need arises, people simply purchase what they need at that time.

So, how do you handle procurement?

- **Centralize the procurement process**. If at all possible, create a central procurement or purchasing office for your worldwide operations. While each region may have its own office of procurement, each of these entities will report back to the central office.
- **Assess each purchase.** Make sure it's in alignment technology standards/policies/procedures. Make sure it supports the actual needs of your organization/group.

Deployment and tracking

Deployment and tracking, tells you who physically has been assigned, and presumably will use the asset. Once deployed, the asset needs to be tracked within the lifecycle status, meaning that the organization must physically account for critical assets and ensure effective use. For active commodity, assets accountability and assignment may be to the same person. For active service or network infrastructure assets, they will tend to be different. For inactive assets, accountability may be the asset team and assignment may be a storage/stock room. Having the data to physically locate an asset closes the loop on accountability and many regulatory requirements.

Tracking is *not* ITAM: tracking versus managing
Asset tracking deals with the physical characteristics of software in support of planning, deployment, operation, support, and service; installation/use data.
Asset management deals with the fiscal (financial and/or contract) details of software as required for financial management, risk management, contract management, and vendor management; ownership data. *Asset tracking is a prerequisite.*

Retirement versus redeployment

Unlike hardware, retiring a software license does not literally mean *"putting it out to pasture"* or sending it out for IT asset disposition. In fact, software that is deployed and identified as not in use or no longer requested is placed in one of two categories:

- **Reharvest**: Can the license be re-used and re-deployed at some point? If so, the license will be put into a queue and *"reharvested"* as needed.
- **Retire**: If the software is no longer in use, are you still paying for the annual maintenance? If so, the license(s) needs to be *"retired"*.

Ongoing management

Once the lifecycle of a software license has been established, each of those licenses must be tracked and managed. At the onset of the SAM program, a central repository was created for all licensing. The software asset lifecycle management process belongs within the confines of the central repository as a method to reliably track and manage software.

As part of the established central repository, the ongoing management process includes:

1. Inventory management
2. Semi-annual or Quarterly or Monthly audit
3. Development of policies, processes and procedures
4. Education and communications program
5. Procurement/purchasing

Questions that should be asked at the onset and throughout the SAM program:

What software are we licensed for?

- Contracts
- License Agreements
- Procurement

What software has been deployed?

- Auto-discovery
- Physical Inventory

What software should be deployed?

- Request Management
- Change/Release management
- Projects
- SAM analysis

Step 4 - L is for legal (or contract management)

While contract management is part of the software asset lifecycle management, the issue is that legal contracts are usually dealt with separately through internal counsel. While legal counsel is a must with any contract, lawyers are only reviewing the contract from a narrow viewpoint—liability. In reality, a software license agreement should be viewed three dimensionally:

- Liability from a legal viewpoint
- Alignment of IT restrictions and allowances in the contract with the business (short-, mid- and long-term)
- Financial terms

At the heart of any SAM program is the ability to truly understand and interpret a software vendor's contract(s)—specifically the Terms & Conditions and the licensing models and changes. The first and foremost fact that any enterprise should understand is that purchasing software from a software vendor does not mean you own the software. It means you are purchasing the rights to use the software within a certain set of conditions, as stated in the contract (normally found in the Terms & Conditions section).

When dealing with software licensing agreements, it is best to:

- Understand compliance and audit terms and conditions
- Identify the legal entity signing the contract
- Support divestitures and transfers of contract rights
- Identify products governed under a contract
- Determine the lines of business and geographic areas covered under a contract
- Understand the transferability of products within a contract
- Differentiate between perpetual and term/subscription software
- Determine maintenance coverage for products at a contract level (versus at the product level)
- Identify if upgrade rights (conversion of purchased version to latest version of product) are provided
- Manage contract expiration, renewal, and notification requirements
- Provide reporting and reconciliation against contracts
- Support financial forecasting

SAM quick tips that work

QUICK TIP 1

Know what you have:

Find the products already in the environment generating data on software:

• *Three or more common*

Investigate centralizing the data

Consider an automated software dictionary that:

• *Groups executables into user-readable titles*

• *Handles suites*

• *Updates continuously*

• *Allows you to add corporate-grown software*

QUICK TIP 2

Consider how you license:

License types easier to manage

Incorporate true-ups into agreements if that is what you have to do anyway

When buying, get them to provide valid electronic proof of purchase

Match licensing to strategic plans:

• *Skipping an upgrade*

• *Moving to a different platform*

• *Spending now to save later, or vice versa*

QUICK TIP 3

Consider how you allocate:

Does everyone really need it?

Harvest unused licenses:

• *Usage statistics*

• *At hardware disposal*

Standardize the environment further, create larger pools to re-deploy

QUICK TIP 4

M and A are Fire Drills:

Opportunity for auditors:

• *Look before you buy*

• *Get ready ahead of audit*

Review *new* contracts:

• Change of name OK or not

• Location specific contracts

• Look for volume discounts and other advantageous details (test licenses, escrow)

<table>
<tr><td>

QUICK TIP 5

Use audit results:

Audit result: More installed than needed, or licensed:

- *Make sure de-installation procedure works*

- *Build a license bank so these over-purchases aren't lost*

Audit result: Good data on one vendor, up to date license count:

- *Use to build SAM, keep these results up to date*

</td><td>

QUICK TIP 6

Negotiate wisely:

Use audit results in future product purchase negotiations:

- *Negotiate better terms, matching your real usage*

- *Make sure proof of ownership is clear (tackle the media problem)*

Negotiate from overall position with vendor, not a single product

Contracts negotiated wisely but put in a drawer – not so wise!

</td></tr>
<tr><td>

QUICK TIP 7

Build a managed software list:

Managed Software List

Strategic Software

Discovered Software

</td><td>

QUICK TIP 8

Next steps:

Analyze and re-prioritize

Purchase Strategy

- *License types to match overall plan or role*

- *Negotiation processes*

Find opportunities to improve compliance or being able to prove compliance

Network with peers in other companies and seek advice from industry professionals

</td></tr>
</table>

Understanding Compliance, Contracts, License Types

Compliance and audit readiness starts with an understanding of software positions (software purchases) and software installations (license usage). A simple reconciliation would directly align the software product's installed title and version to the software purchase record with the same title and version. This is complicated by a number of factors. For example, software may cover multiple versions of a product, and an installation record may not directly correlate to usage (for example, multiple installs on a single machine covered by a single license).

Contracts provide additional governing rules and terms to product usage. Geographic and line of business restrictions further segment the rights of a particular license and its applicability to an installation. Contracts may also provide additional rights including upgrades to licenses, which in turn would provide increased use rights to a product that can be applied to additional installs of products at a higher version level than purchased.

Creating a license and installation position (effective license position) based on software product-level use rights and contractual terms is critical to assuring compliance and an increase efficiency of licensing. Efficiency of licensing is the result of avoiding unnecessary license purchases. An audit risk is present when the effective license position is not understood.

The relationship between software and contracts

Contracts specify the software products that are governed by the contractual terms. Contractual purchases identify licenses purchased (software assets) to a contract. Purchases processed through standard systems (for example, P2P) might not specify the contracts in which a software asset is purchased against. This is why it is key to track your contracts along with your software products and installations in an ITAM/SAM tool. You will need to identify the software products governed by the contract. This is used for audit and compliance to assure the proper terms and rights are applied to the software products specified in the contract.

Contract hierarchy

Vendor contracts may consist of multiple contract documents, including top-level agreements (commonly referred to as master agreements), exhibits, schedules, addendums, and appendices.

A contract hierarchy consists of all of the documents that uniquely address a single contractual arrangement. Modifying documents, including schedules, addendums, and appendices, are created as children to the top-level agreement.

Child agreements to the top-level contract may identify the addition of products or removal of products.

Child contracts (these can include master agreements, schedules, addendums, and appendices) that modify a top-level agreement (for example, removal of a covered product or addition of a covered product) must indicate that they modify the top-level agreement for querying and reporting purposes.

Software contracts and licensing types

Key elements of a software or software maintenance contract include:

- License or maintenance
- ELA, End User License Agreement/EULA, Master License Agreement, SLA, and VPA
- Perpetual, term, or subscription

Types of Software Licenses:

Here are some software license definitions. I could never fully cover them all. That would entail a whole book of itself. All software vendors have different license models and structures. I have designed to cover the most popular and some of the less known licensing schemes adopted by software publishers.

Nodelocked Licenses	Network Licenses	Simple Nodelocked
Concurrent	Concurrent Nodelocked	Concurrent-offline
Use-Once Nodelocked	Reservable	Per-server
Use-Once	Per-Seat	Freeware
Limited License	Unlimited Site License	Volume Licensing
Perpetual License	Shareware	Subscription License
Enterprise License	TrueUp	Term
Unlimited	Unlimited-capped	
Single-User	Named Licenses	

Perpetual is a license to use the software indefinitely. The license is paid for once and does not need to be renewed.

The software may be governed by a specified contract or by the product's standard license agreement. Maintenance contracts may provide for additional product rights, including upgrade rights to future versions that effectively change the underlying license.

Term

Term is a license to use the software for a specified period of time. The license is paid for the initial term and has a recurring payment for additional terms. This license expires at the end of the specified term and requires an additional term or new license to continue usage of the product.

The software may be governed by a specified contract that includes, at a minimum, the term of usage. The software's usage will be further governed by the software license agreement or terms specified in the contract. Maintenance is generally included with these licenses rather than being covered under separate maintenance agreements. Term licenses generally provide use-rights to future versions of the products.

Subscription

Subscription is a license that allows users to use the software for a specified period of time. This license usually includes technical support and access to upgrades and patches released during the term of the subscription. At the end of the term, the user has several options: renew the subscription or purchase a perpetual license at a discounted cost (if offered) or remove the software from the device.

Enterprise License

This type of license allows a company to have either an unlimited use license for all their applications or a limited amount per contract. This entitles the company and its subsidiaries regardless of location, unlimited use for a specified period of time for a specified value.

Unlimited Site License

This license enables a certain location (site) of your organization to have unlimited use license for a specific piece of software as dictated by the contract agreement.

Freeware License

This license type is offered as freeware by the author and does not require paying any fee for use. It is considered public domain; there are no copyright restrictions. It can be copied and distributed freely. However, make sure to read their terms. At times, freeware is not always free if used for commercial purposes.

Limited License

An agreement whereby software is purchased with limits and/or restrictions on the number of copies available for installation or use. Limited licenses are sometimes limited to a designated number of devices.

Volume Licensing

Allows the licensee to install the software on a certain number of devices. The licensee usually has to satisfy a minimum purchase requirement and obtain reduced prices in exchange. A good example of volume licensing is the Microsoft Products and Services Agreement (MPSA).

Shareware

Shareware also called trialware or demoware is proprietary software that is provided to users on a limited basis and only for a certain limited trial/evaluation period. It is copyrighted software that a developer encourages you to copy and distribute. This permission is explicitly stated in the documentation.

Nodelocked Licenses

Nodelocked licenses allow the use of software on the particular machine for which the license was created for as long as the license remains valid. Vendors typically use nodelocked licenses for standalone, rather than client/server, applications.

A vendor who is enabling a software product using nodelocked licenses can choose between two license-enabling models: *non-runtime-based* and *runtime-based.*

If the vendor chooses non-runtime-based enabling, the license-enabled software product will not need the License Use Runtime to be installed. The password for such a software product is stored in a file called the *nodelock file.* The application checks the nodelock file to be sure a valid license is available.

If the vendor chooses runtime-based enabling, management of the nodelocked license is performed by the *nodelocked license server* on the local machine. The nodelocked license server is managed through the BLT, Basic License Tool, which enables you to view and update information about the nodelocked licenses on the machine and get reports about their use.

Vendors can enable their software products using the following kinds of nodelocked licenses:

- Simple nodelocked licenses
- Concurrent nodelocked licenses
- Use-once nodelocked licenses
- Per-server licenses

Simple Nodelocked Licenses

Simple nodelocked licenses allow an unlimited number of simultaneous uses of the licensed application on the local machine. Simple nodelocked licenses are valid only for vendor-managed use products. A word processor is a typical example of a nodelocked licensed product.

Concurrent Nodelocked Licenses

As with a simple nodelocked license, concurrent nodelocked licenses are local to the node where the application has been installed. It allows a limited number of simultaneous uses of the licensed application. A typical example of a concurrent nodelocked license is a client/server application, where the application server is able to recognize the number of clients connected to it and ask for a license for each of them.

Vendors can use concurrent nodelocked licenses for both vendor-managed and customer-managed products. If the product is customer-managed, when you enroll the product, you must specify how many concurrent nodelocked licenses you have acquired for the product. The end user can modify this number at any time.

Use-Once Nodelocked Licenses

Use-once nodelocked licenses permit a single use of a particular licensed product on a particular machine within the period for which the license is valid. Every time the product is started, one license is consumed.

A typical use of use-once nodelocked licenses is to distribute promotional or demonstration versions of software.

Vendors also provide use-once nodelocked licenses to supplement concurrent nodelocked licenses during times when user demand for those products exceeds the number of available concurrent nodelocked licenses. The vendor designs the product so that when all concurrent nodelocked licenses for the product are in use, a user can request an available use-once license.

Vendors can use use-once nodelocked licenses for both vendor-managed and customer-managed products. If the product is customer-managed, when you enroll the licenses, you must specify how many use-once nodelocked licenses you have acquired for the product. The end user can modify this number at any time.

Per-Server Licenses

Per-server licenses are exactly like concurrent nodelocked licenses, except that at any time, you can change them into per-seat licenses.

Vendors use per-server/per-seat licenses to enable client/server applications constructed for multiple-server solutions. Both per-server and per-seat licenses make it possible for the server of a licensed client/server application to request licenses on behalf of its clients without the need for the application clients to be license-enabled.

With per-server licensing, each application server license is associated with a specific number of application clients, representing the maximum number of application clients that may concurrently request services from that application server. The application client licenses are stored locally on the application server machine and are granted temporarily to requesting application clients. Multiple application servers grant licenses independently of one another; if the same application client connects to more than one application server, the application client is granted more than one license. It is recommended to use per-server licenses only in an environment where:

- Each application client connects to only a single application server
- Each application client uses the application infrequently for brief periods.

When your environment grows in such a way that application clients are connecting to multiple application servers, you will probably want to convert your per-server licenses to per-seat. With per-seat licensing, unused application client licenses are kept in a central repository, which all the application servers share. They also share a central list of application clients to which a license has been assigned. When a license is assigned to an application client, that assignment is permanent. If an application client connects to multiple application servers, it is assigned only one license.

Per-server licenses are valid only for customer-managed use products.

Network Licenses

Network licenses are not restricted to a single machine. They are stored on a network license server and shared among multiple network license clients.

Vendors can enable their software products using the following kinds of network licenses:

- Concurrent licenses
- Concurrent-offline licenses
- Reservable licenses
- Use-once licenses
- Per-seat licenses

Concurrent Licenses

Concurrent licenses are network licenses that can be temporarily granted to run the licensed application on a client.

When the software product is running, that license remains unavailable to other users of the product. When the product stops running the license is returned to the server, where it becomes available to other users.

Concurrent licenses allow as many users to run a licensed software application simultaneously as there are valid licenses for the product available from the network license servers in your licensing environment.

A typical use of concurrent licenses is for software with relatively expensive licenses that each user will use only part of the time. You order fewer licenses than there are users to optimize use of the licenses. Such applications may be client/server applications for which the client is enabled, or non-client/server applications.

Vendors can use concurrent licenses for both vendor-managed and customer-managed products.

Reservable Licenses

Reservable licenses are network license that you can reserve for the exclusive use of a user, a group, or a node. The reservation is for a specified time period. A reservable license that has been reserved is called a reserved license. A reservable license that has not been reserved is called an unreserved license.

When a reserved license is granted from the network, the license is stored on the workstation where the licensed application is running. Thereafter, the license can be used on the workstation, even if the workstation is disconnected from the network, until the reservation expires.

A typical use of reservable licenses is for the client part of a client/server application that is likely to run on a portable computer that is often disconnected from the network. Another typical use is for a compiler being used in software development. During a build process involving many compilations, it is more efficient to reserve a compiler license for a day or two than to make a separate request for a compiler license for every compilation.

You can reserve some of the reservable licenses for an application and leave others unreserved. Unreserved licenses are treated like concurrent licenses.

Vendors can use reservable licenses for both vendor-managed and customer-managed products.

Use-Once Licenses

Use-once licenses are network licenses that permits a single use of a particular licensed product within the period for which the license is valid. Every time the product is started, one license is consumed.

A typical use of use-once licenses is to distribute promotional or demonstration versions of software.

Vendors also provide use-once licenses for their products to supplement concurrent licenses during times when user demand for those products exceeds the number of available concurrent licenses. The vendor designs the product so that when all concurrent licenses for the product are in use, a user can request an available use-once license.

Vendors can use use-once licenses for both vendor-managed and customer-managed products.

Per-Seat Licenses

Vendors use per-server/per-seat licenses to enable client/server applications constructed for multiple-server solutions. Both per-server and per-seat licenses make it possible for the server of a licensed client/server application to request licenses on behalf of its clients without the need for the application clients to be license-enabled.

With per-seat licensing, unused application client licenses are kept in a central repository, which all the application servers share. They also share a central list of application clients to which a license has been assigned. When a license is assigned to an application client, that assignment is permanent. If an application client connects to multiple application servers, it is assigned only one license.

You will probably want to use per-seat, rather than per-server, licenses in an environment where application clients connect to multiple application servers. (See also "Per-Server Licenses".).

Per-seat licenses are valid only for customer-managed use products.

Key contract attributes for unlimited license usage include **True Up**, **Unlimited**, and **Unlimited Capped**. This attribute is used to determine counting logic for software products covered by these contract types.

True Up

A True Up based contract allows for unlimited usage of products specified within the contract but requires payments for additional deployments (net increase in installations) at specified dates during the contract term. Under-licensed positions for products covered by these contract types are addressed at the True Up dates.

Unlimited

Unlimited is a unique license that applies to products within a contract. The specified products can be used by any number of users or on any number of machines during the contract term. Additional usage or deployment of named products during the term of the unlimited license agreement will not incur additional charges.

The software will be governed by a specified contract that includes, at a minimum, the conditions for the end of contract (conversion to perpetual or term licenses, additional payments, and so on). The product's usage will be further governed by the product's license agreement or terms specified in the contract.

Maintenance may be included in an unlimited license agreement. Most unlimited license agreements will require maintenance to be provided for all deployed products. Unlimited licenses generally provide use-rights to future versions of the products or are specified at the product without version restrictions.

The Unlimited license type should be leveraged in the reconciliation process. Any license that has a contract with an Unlimited classification will not result in an under-license condition for the products covered by the contract. This applies for the licenses within the contract coverage area.

Unlimited-Capped

Unlimited licenses may include a usage cap or ceiling. These license agreements are consistent with Unlimited but provide for a *not to exceed* clause limiting a product's deployment.

The Unlimited-Capped license type should be leveraged in the reconciliation process via a purchase record or records. Asset (purchase) record(s) should be created with the maximum number of allowed licenses by contract. The licenses should be set to expire at the contract end date. At the expiration of the contract, new asset records should be produced for the remaining licenses (those converted to perpetual or term), identifying any expiration or conditions on the *replacement* licenses.

Contracts with an unlimited type generally have reporting dates associated with them. These dates may include True Up dates, end of contract usage reporting, or other reporting requirements as stipulated in the contract.

Contract coverage

A vendor/supplier generally instantiates an audit, formally or informally, by stating that they believe there is an "out of compliance" position against a contract. However, the effective license position may include software product usage across multiple contracts. Software reconciliation processes should therefore apply contractual terms and contract coverage restrictions across all contracts affecting the effective license position of all products included in an audit. We will learn more about software audits in `Chapter 5,` *Understanding and Surviving Software License Compliance Audits*.

My overall goal is to help you understand how to apply contractual terms and contract coverage restrictions across all contracts affecting the effective license position of all software products included in an audit. To understand that software reconciliation is achieved by determining the software purchase position by contract and install position by software product. The benefits are improved license management for your organization resulting in improved reporting, audit compliance, cost savings, and proactive instead of reactive responses to vendor audits, as well as meet your organization's business needs.

How Does Transferability Affect Licenses?

Improperly transferring licenses results in a compliance issue that may result in additional licensing fees and penalties.

The ability to transfer license rights has financial implications under the following scenarios:

- Transfer to outsourcing provider
- Transfer to divested entity
- Transfer from divested entity (licensee legal entity) to retained entity
- Sale of software to a third-party

Software licenses generally limit transferability. Lack of transferability increases the cost of divestiture, requiring additional licensing for the divested company and creating a glut of additional licenses for the retained companies. Additional licensing terms, including pricing, may be less favorable for the divested company, further increasing the divestiture costs.

If the divested company owns the contract and licenses without transferability, the divested company may be stuck with a glut of licenses and create a gap and licensing requirements for retained entities covered by the contract's licenses.

Upgrades

Software upgrades are available for many products at a reduced cost to full licenses or as a component of maintenance agreements, whether purchased individually for a product or included in a contract. The focus here is on contract handling. However, a base understanding of upgrade scenarios and processing is key to understanding how contract rights can be applied.

Upgrades for software licenses can be provided at the software asset level through an upgrade license purchase, a software product purchased with upgrade rights (for example, software assures), or through contract level rights.

 Each upgrade plus a base license constitutes a single license for a new product version.

Upgrade license purchase

Upgraded licenses (software assets) are counted towards full license rights. Upgraded base licenses are not counted in reconciliation processing. Maintain a linkage/record to provide proof of licensing. I carry out quite a few audit reviews, especially reviewing audit findings of vendors for companies. It is always a battle when it comes to upgrade licenses with no proof of the base license. Save yourself the headache and track both and link them together. Track the following in an ITAM/SAM tool:

- Upgrade purchased
- Base software asset identified (coverage, cost center, lowest version level supported by upgrade, and so on)
- Base software asset status changed to *Upgraded*
- Upgrade license linked to base license

For example, an upgrade purchase that specifies the software product to be upgraded will trigger a workflow to identify a covered software asset to be converted to Upgraded status. A lack of available software assets for upgrade will trigger an exception process for manual assignment or a requirement to purchase a valid covered base license.

This process assures both compliance and the effective assignment of upgrades (the version upgrade purchased is applied to the lowest level base license or to the version the contract states).

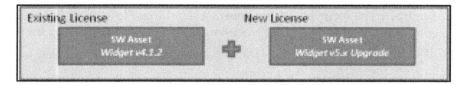

An example of version update

 Proof of license entitlement requires purchase data for both the base license and the upgrade license

License purchase provides upgrade rights

Some products include upgrade rights with the license purchase. These may include:

- Updates included (minor and maintenance releases)
- Upgrades included for a period of time (upgrade limited to term)
- Upgrades included up to a certain version level (for example, next major version release; but may also be time limited)
- Version rights during the term (version not specified at purchase; fixed at end of the upgrade term)

Contracts providing software product upgrades

Maintenance contracts can provide upgrade rights for a group of software products. This is similar to an individual maintenance with an upgrade item; however a contract has a one-to-many relationship with products. This type of contract acts like a bundle in that it provides these rights to a set of products associated with the agreement.

Contracts that provide upgrade rights can use an automated workflow to create upgraded licenses based on contract conditions (for example, renewal dates) or be queried for upgrade rights by product coverage.

Software associated with a contract does not need to be updated when a contract is extended. The revised dates of coverage are changed in the contract and flow down to the covered products. Upgrades processed will follow the upgrade license purchase process defined previously. The new software asset will be linked to the maintenance contract.

Contracts providing software product upgrades for unlimited use products

Unlimited use contracts where the assets are not created (for example, term contracts) will not require upgrade processing. The reconciliation process will support any version of the product.

Unlimited contracts converted to perpetual licenses will be created at the end-of-contract version level. No additional upgrade processing is required.

True Up contracts will have asset records with a version of SA. This will follow the process just described for individual support contracts; however, the assets will link to the maintenance contract instead of the individual maintenance product purchase.

Contract reconciliation and reporting

Contract reporting includes control, summary, and reconciliation reports. These reports provide contract coverage of products, product or contract level views, reconciliation of products against contracts, and contract views of supported products.

Contract level reporting incorporates contract coverage (geographical and **Line of Business (LOB)**) to assure compliance and maximize license efficiency. For example, 100 licenses of a product applied to 100 installations may show a compliant reconciliation position. However, if the 100 licenses are from contracts that do not provide coverage for 20 of the installations, the actual position would be a license deficit of 20 licenses.

Contract reconciliation reports and software product/contract control reports provide key information for quickly addressing audit requests and understanding license positions for contract renewal or negotiations.

As products are associated with contracts, the situation arises where there will be:

- Products covered by a single contract
- Products covered by multiple contracts
- Products not covered by a contract

The three categories of reporting provide:

- **Control reports**: Overview of total contracts and product coverage of contracts
- **Contract coverage reports**: Overview of contracts segmented by geographical coverage, and line-of-business coverage
- **Reconciliation reports**: Identification of software over- or under-license conditions by contract or product

Contract level reconciliation reporting occurs at the master contract level. All schedules, appendices, and addendums associated with a contract roll-up to the master contract level. Reconciling at the contract roll-up level incorporates all additions, changes, and deletions associated with child contracts, assuring an accurate compliance view.

A key to reporting and reconciliation at the contract level is having a clear understanding and approach to associating licenses (purchases) to contracts, and associating installs to licenses (via contract).

Summary

This chapter has covered software asset management, some of the standards and frameworks that exist, and real-world results when SAM is implemented successfully. While I've outlined 4 critical and foundational steps for implementing a good SAM program, the last step is savings. Gartner, Forrester, and many other industry researchers have stated that organizations can realize a cost savings of 20 to 35% by implementing a SAM program in its first year.

Having an ongoing SAM program plays into a number of proactive and reactive scenarios, such as:

- **Vendor Audit Preparedness**: Software vendors can and will audit their customers at any time. With a SAM program, running a product-level reconciliation report will provide a reliable compliance picture.
- **Contract Renewal**: SAM helps to automate and manage any contracts up for renewal so that well-negotiated Terms & Conditions are not lost due to an oversight of not re-upping on time.

- **Business Change**: SAM can help with any sudden (or maybe not so sudden) business changes - mergers, acquisitions, or divestitures - by providing reports on current licensing positions. This can be used to create an effective strategy to cover any licensing and compliance gaps, or even to create short- or long-term savings.
- **Licensing Negotiations**: People often mistakenly assume that licensing negotiations only happen during an initial purchase or at the time of True Up. Licensing negotiations can happen throughout the year for any reason - from senior executives seeking to cut costs by 15-20% to migration projects to any modification in business. An ongoing, well-run SAM program enables and empowers the enterprise to easily access information necessary to negotiate the best deals for the best values.
- **Shelfware:** SAM can help with overspending. Shelfware is a term given to software that has been purchased but never used. Typically, purchased because of a perceived need or future demand, or to obtain a great discount. Your SAM program allows you to proactively manage your software and monitor usage of that software. It allows you to have a clear picture of usage; if the software is actually being used and if you have software not being used at all. You can than make informed decisions on what steps to take with your shelfware. One approach not many know to try is with usage data in hand, negotiate contracts at renewal time to bring the number of licenses you hold down to what you really need.

Bottom line: there is a long list of IT and operational events that a SAM program plays into and the vast majority results in cost savings, operational efficiency, and/or lower risk.

Usage	Contracts	Process
➢ Which applications are not in use? ➢ Which applications are over-licensed when compare to use? ➢ Should the standard image be adjusted? ➢ Are there products in use that have the same functionality? ➢ Are technology enhancements changing how usage is occurring (virtualization, CITRIX, and so on.) ➢ Does the organizational structure allow re-purposing of licenses and if so, does it occur?	➢ Is there more than one contract for a specific application and are savings possible through consolidation? ➢ Are there untapped savings opportunities in current contacts such as site licensing, enterprise licensing, moving to a small server? ➢ Can negotiations practices by updated to generate savings, immediate or long term? ➢ What costs are associated with each vendor and application?	➢ Are any SAM processes missing or out of compliance with ISO 19770-1? ➢ Is the corporate software policy up to date, complete, and enforceable? ➢ Does the life cycle process re-capture licenses at hardware disposal? ➢ Is there an awareness campaign for all users? ➢ Are there desktop lock-down capabilities that can be used to improve compliance?

In the next chapter, you will learn how to survive a software audit and what steps to take once you receive the dreaded audit demand letter.

5
Understanding and Surviving Software License Compliance Audits

Vendor audits are on the rise and the future outlook is that they will continue to increase, especially as vendors realize that the return on investment in a customer compliance program brings back an average of ten dollars for every dollar spent. More focus will be placed on compliance from both the vendor and the end-user perspectives.

We've already seen an increase in government compliance regulation in the form of the **Sarbanes-Oxley Act (SOX)**, the **Graham-Leach-Bliley Act (GLBA)**, and the **Health Information Portability and Accountability Act (HIPAA)**, all of which have some level of IT governance written into them.

So, with the increase in compliance activity that is going on in the business world, is there anything that you can do to avoid a license compliance event in the future? Not really, short of not buying software to help run your business, but who can afford to do that? Vendor compliance audits are fast becoming inevitable for mid- to large-sized companies.

Reducing impact

You may not be able to avoid a software license compliance audit, but you can start now to reduce the impact that an audit may have on your organization by implementing some best practices for **software asset management (SAM)**. These practices can reduce some of the red flags that non-compliant companies reveal to those vendors who audit.

SAM best practices:

- Established policies and processes for how software is used, distributed and managed within the enterprise.
- A software discovery method/tool for determining what is installed and/or being used throughout the enterprise.
- A central repository for storing and linking software license data (contracts, purchase records, and so on) to hardware and software assets.
- A periodically scheduled self-audit process rooted in the same methodologies used by vendor auditors that allow you to address any over and under licensing. The added benefit to this is cost control.
- Centralized procurement processes to eliminate the many ways that software (and other assets) can be over or under purchased
- A goal to negotiate better software license agreements, rather than accepting the stock *boilerplate* contract that a vendor will offer.

License Compliance Audit Triggers:

- *If something smells fishy, it probably is.* The *smell test* concept is a universal concept that applies to license compliance. If something with a customer does not seem right to an account manager, it probably isn't and should be looked into.
- Conflicting/Correcting statements such as *last week I told you I thought we were using 500 licenses, but I found out that we are using only 350*. Why the difference? What changed? What method did you use to arrive at that count? These are questions you should be prepared to answer if you make conflicting statements to a vendor account manager.
- Most end users want the increased functionality that comes with using the most recent version of a software product. Unwillingness to upgrade to a more current version may come across as suspicious, as a validation of licenses in use usually accompanies an upgrade or purchase of upgrade licenses.
- There may be a perception among end-users that they can overcome a shortfall in licenses by changing the licensing model under which they are purchasing and may request to explore other licensing models. Most publishers will automatically desire an audit in this situation, as they have set metrics for determining the exchange of licenses from one model to another and will need to determine what is currently in use to accomplish this.

- Upward shifts in the employee base, with no accompanying purchase order are another red flag. The acquisition or merger of two companies often becomes public knowledge, as does any company growth. Most companies like to toot their horn with this positive news and a good account manager will be on top of changes to their client base like this. Usually, more employees translate to more licenses being required to use the software and the vendor will be expecting a dialogue to address this.

In the end, the more a vendor account manager knows about and is involved with your efforts to manage your software licenses, the better off you are. The idea behind this is that the more a software vendor knows about your internal compliance initiatives, the less likely they will be to initiate an unexpected audit of your contract, as the expense will be perceived as unnecessary! By implementing these changes and addressing these issues, you can be much better prepared for the inevitable vendor audit.

Understanding the risks of non-compliance

Before reviewing the steps that need to be taken in the event of an unwanted software audit, enterprise leaders should be aware of the risks involved. There is nothing fun about a software audit and the best an enterprise can hope for is that it is in compliance, so that mostly the enterprise's time was drained. At worst, an audit may find an enterprise out of compliance, which carries significant costs in time, monetary penalties, possible third-party legal and IT fees, and potentially additional software expenditures. Unless a company can prove otherwise, the assumption is that every infringement was willful, and penalties of up to $250,000 in statutory damages can be charged for each infringement. Furthermore, the costs can also include the recovery of the software vendor's attorneys' fees under 17 U.S.C. §505 of the Federal Code. In large organizations, these costs can add up to millions of dollars in a hurry.

Beyond the direct financial costs involved, software audits also impact organizations by disrupting the normal flow of business efforts, drawing resources away from meeting the needs of the company's customers. The financial impact of an audit may include damage to your brand reputation, with additional marketing costs to recover from negative publicity.

Many organizations are blissfully unconcerned about potential audits because they have policies that forbid the installation and use of unauthorized software. What they may not understand is that any enterprise can unwittingly fall out of licensing compliance over time for a variety of reasons – annual changes in licensing rules, software company mergers, true-up clauses in your licensing agreements, the addition or updating of servers, consolidation of architecture, expansion into new geographies, outsourcing, web-enabled applications. The list goes on and on!

This is why so many organizations have recently invested in ITAM and SAM programs that effectively manage, control, and track software assets throughout the enterprise during all stages of their lifecycle. A good SAM program helps organizations remain in compliance in the first place, and greatly simplifies the burdensome process of a software audit. However, whether you have a SAM process in place or not, the critical steps and issues to resolve during a software audit remain essentially the same.

The audit response plan – steps to take when the gotcha letter arrives

There are two things that enterprise leaders can be certain of today: taxes and unwanted software audit in the near future.

Software is intellectual property and vendors guard their rights to it seriously. Even if you haven't been audited before, or even if you've been audited last year, you must understand that software vendor audits are inevitable and now a part of doing business. So, what do you do when you get that first demand letter?

First, understand that this demand letter was unavoidable.

Unwanted, of course, but a software audit should no longer be unexpected. The number of software vendor audits has been increasing for the last 10 years now as a means of ensuring full compliance with licensing terms, and, of course, full payment for current software usage. Software is a revenue-generating activity for many (though not all) software companies. It is also a means to protect their intellectual property, and vendors guard their rights fiercely—it is the life's blood of their business.

The dreaded, inevitable demand letter from a software vendor or an IT compliance agency lands on your desk. Now what? To start with the obvious: don't panic, don't ignore it, don't admit or deny the allegations, and don't discard the letter or hope it will go away.

Whether you are ultimately in compliance or not, this is not the end of the world... but you will need help: legal guidance, your internal SMEs, and possibly third-party IT consultants with experience in handling software audits and negotiating favorable resolutions.

Bear in mind that, although relationships between software publishers and their customers is becoming increasingly confrontational, software companies generally want to avoid litigation and ruinous penalties as much as their enterprise customers. Remedies and penalties are always negotiable, especially if they expect your company to be a long-term, ongoing customer.

Here is a typical audit letter your organization can receive:

January 2, 20XX

First Name, Last Name
Manager
Company ABC
Address 1
Address 2
City, State, Zip

Re: Vendor X Software License Review

Dear First Name, Last Name:

We would like to express our appreciation to Company ABC for utilizing Vendor X technology solutions within your enterprise.

The Company ABC has been selected to undergo a Vendor X software license review. Vendor X License & Compliance ("L&C") works with our customers to conduct objective software license reviews to ensure that Vendor X software is being utilized in compliance with the terms and conditions of the End User License Agreements ("EULA"). Software license reviews are part of Vendor X's continuous efforts to highlight the importance of software asset management and to improve our overall licensing programs.

In an effort to expedite the software license review and add value to your existing software asset management practices, Vendor X has created a multi-step review process, as outlined on the next page. I will contact you within five business days to conduct our first meeting. Vendor X values our relationship with Company ABC System and we appreciate your attention to this matter. I look forward to working with you.

Sincerely yours,

Full Name, Senior License Compliance Consultant
Phone:
E-mail: |

Software License Review Process

The Vendor X software license review process is comprised of the following standard procedures, including but not limited to:

1. Company ABC System's completion of the attached **Environment Worksheet**, which will help determine the scope of the review. Please be prepared to discuss these worksheets in detail at our initial conference call, to be set within five business days of the date of this letter.

2. Submission of an **Active Directory hardware report** exported via the Windows based CSVDE command tool (see attached instructions). This tool needs to be run on each domain within your organization (if more than one). This report(s) is due to Vendor X within 15 days of the date of this letter.

3. Submission of **two installation data reports** from your specified Software Asset Management (SAM) tool or Vendor X scan tool (if needed) for all regions deemed within scope, as agreed upon during the phone conference. These reports are due to Vendor X within 30 days of the date of this letter and will include the following:

   - Desktop data - for all workstations in your organization
   - Server data - supplemented by the Vendor X Environment Worksheet

4. Submission of all **additional purchase data**, including data from your resellers, for all related entity names, for all regions, for all available historic dates, within 30 days of the date of this letter. To ensure completeness, please include the most data possible and go back in time as far as the reports allow.

5. Upon complete submission of the above deliverables, Vendor X will compare your software deployment with your license purchases and the terms of the associated EULAs. Vendor X will submit to you a **findings report** including complete license reconciliation for your records.

6. If the above analysis shows a deficit in licensing, we will ask that you work with your Vendor X Account Manager and/or your reseller of choice to resolve any compliance findings by **purchasing the deficient licenses** immediately and no later than 14 days from the notification of findings by Vendor X.

Please prepare to make all supporting records available upon request. These steps will help to ensure an efficient review process as well as proper licensing for your organization. We have also enclosed a document containing frequently asked questions for your review.

Once you've received the audit notification letter, the following steps should be taken to disseminate, cooperate, aggregate, and mitigate for this and future audits:

1. **Evaluate**: Determine the current state of audit preparedness by addressing the following:

    - **Software policies**: Having enforceable policies that address the usage of software within the company and that control how and what software is installed.

    - **Procurement processes**: Having policies that address the *who, what, why, when and how* of the acquisition of software, as well as the accessibility of purchasing data to those who will need it.

    - **Self-audit procedures**: Having the means and procedures to be able to compare what has been purchased to what is being used, as well as knowing the terms and conditions that are compliance-related in their contracts and software license agreements.

    - **Internal contact information**: Are the proper people to be involved in a vendor audit identified and have they been notified? Is there an assigned audit team consisting of people from the various departments upon which the audit will touch?

- **Vendor management**: Knowing which vendors audit can help to prepare for an audit from those companies specifically. Letting the various account managers know that the company is working to improve their software license compliance procedures will also help to mitigate the audit risk.

2. **Disseminate**: There are certain internal organizational entities that must be notified when a software audit is imminent, so as to give them time to prepare for it and assign a person to be a part of the audit response team.
    - **Legal**: Whether it is internal or external, your legal department should be notified and given a copy of the audit notification letter. They are in the best position to counsel on what legal steps there may be to lessen the impact of the audit process. Hopefully, they have experience in software licensing and can add that experience to the process.
    - **IT management**: IT management that is not aware of the audit, but ought to be notified may include senior management up to the CIO level. Systems and/or Network administrators may need to be notified if their systems will be impacted by the audit process.
    - **Senior management**: Depending on our corporate culture and how involved senior management wants to be, you may need to notify even the CEO of an upcoming audit.
    - **Purchasing**: Both internal procurement staff and external software fulfillment agents need to be notified so that they can provide the relevant purchase data for proof of license ownership. The vendor will bring their own purchase data, but do not count on their data to be accurate. It is quite possible that you may show information in your files that adds to what they will bring, as fulfillment agents do not always pass on the purchase information back to the vendor in a timely manner.

3. **Cooperate**: Being cooperative throughout the audit process will make the process go more smoothly and have less impact on your time and business. Of course, that does not mean you should agree to everything the auditors ask of you, but you should weigh carefully your responses to reasonable requests and avoid an escalation of rhetoric based on an emotional response. The auditors have a process to follow that may be flexible and it may not, depending on the vendor. It's more or less the same process they use for all of their customers. Working cooperatively with them to accomplish the scope of their audit eliminates the red flag that is being thrown when unreasonable responses are the result of reasonable requests.

- **Schedule audit date**: There may be a requested audit date or range of dates in the notification letter, but these are still usually negotiable. Find a date that works best for you and offer it, or a range of alternatives, as a counter-proposal to the auditors. At times, on-site audits are scheduled in the same geographic area to reduce travel costs and maximize the usage of time by the auditors and there may be less flexibility in a situation like that, so be prepared for this type of response to your counter-proposal.
- **Be responsive to inquiries**: Giving the same courtesy of a quick response to inquiries by the auditors that you would give to any of your customers can go a long way to building that level of trust you want during the audit process.
- **Ask lots of questions**: Knowing what is in store for you throughout the audit process helps to ease your own mind and can help to set up your expectations of what the final result will be of the audit. The auditors should provide some information about their process and scope, but be prepared to ask lots of questions to fill in any gaps you may feel are there.

4. **Aggregate**: Having at hand all of the relevant information to prove your case is essential to your audit preparation activities.
    - **Collect purchase records**: As mentioned, your purchase history is absolutely essential to proving what you've purchased and are entitled to use.
    - **Collect proofs of purchase**: Any proofs of purchase you have (Certificates of Authenticity, purchase invoices, license certificates, etc.) need to be gathered in case they are asked for.
    - **Contract/software license agreement**: Obtaining a copy of your contract and/or software license agreement puts you on even ground with the auditors, as the audit scope is always determined by the contract you have with the vendor. The contract is the audit baseline.

5. **Mitigate**: Reducing the impact of the audit on your business operations as much as possible, as well as reducing the risk that future audits are going to negatively impact your business is the goal of mitigation.
    - **Self-audit**: Conduct a self-audit to give yourself a heads up on what may be an approximate outcome of the audit. Self-auditing should also be an integral part of any license management program and will do much to maintain compliance on a go-forward basis.

- **Audit response team**: Assign an audit response team and a point of contact for the audit process. This person is responsible to acquire what the auditors need, for all communication, and to liaise between various parties within the company.
- **Frontloading**: Reducing the audit's impact on your business through frontloading the audit process. This means that you do as much as possible before the auditors actually arrive on-site. For instance, if there are documents to be provided, send them to the auditors and if there is data to be collected, collect it and send it to the auditors for processing. Don't wait until they arrive. Through frontloading, your *opening meeting* could actually turn into a *closing meeting* because all of the work was done before the auditors arrived.

Why were you targeted for an audit?

It may have been a disgruntled employee out for revenge, or a software vendor decided it was your turn, or perhaps an IT compliance agency selected your enterprise as part of a random series of audits. It doesn't really matter - one way or another, it was your turn. The bottom line is that routine, periodic audits are the only way for software companies to ensure full payment for their intellectual property. Demand letters from software vendors or IT compliance agencies such as the Business Software Alliance (BSA) are inevitable these days. An audit is not a question of "if?" but "when?"

It is of little surprise, then, that industry analyst Gartner, Inc. recently reported that 35 percent of the companies responding to a survey indicated that they have undergone an on-site, software publisher-initiated audit. That percentage will grow rapidly in coming years, and far too many enterprises are unaware of the deep impact a software audit can have - financially, and in terms of time consumed, and productivity lost.

Caution

Audits are not always formal and do not always appear via letter or email. Sometimes vendors reach out to you under the pretense of updating you about their new products, asking probing questions about your business, rather than inquiring on the use of their software within your environment. You should ask them if this is an audit outright. You will be surprised to find out it is the beginning of one and should treat it as such.

What's your level of non-compliance risk?

Is your organization in danger of being out of compliance with your software licensing agreements? Before dismissing this threat, or pushing the panic button, enterprise leaders should consider a short list of questions prepared by leading industry consultant. Gartner, Inc., to determine if their organization is at a high risk of non-compliance with their software licensing:

- How long has it been since a meeting was held on contract compliance and asset management?
- Does the CIO know who is responsible for ITAM?
- Are personnel trained in software license negotiation managing the technology contracts?
- Is there centralized technology procurement within the enterprise?
- How long has it been since a desktop audit was performed?
- Are asset management projects funded?
- Does the enterprise have written procedures on software procurement processes?
- Does the enterprise have written policies on software licenses that are not legally procured?

Gartner suggests that if your answer to any of these questions is *no* or *I don't know*, then your enterprise has a high risk of noncompliance.

A few questions I would add to this list:

- Does your IT department have the tools it needs to maintain a comprehensive view of your IT estate, including software and hardware, to help determine how the software is being used and whether you are in compliance?
- Do you have an effective SAM program in place to help monitor compliance?
- Do you have a good software disaster recovery plan in place that can periodically update a centralized repository offsite to mirror your onsite software estate?

Again, if the answer to any of these is *no* you should start implementing systems, policies and procedures to protect your enterprise from worst-case audit scenarios. An ounce of prevention can save many pounds of enforced cures.

A special look at the Vendor/Auditor License Compliance Review process

The License Compliance Review process of vendors and auditors is broken down into 5 phases. Due to the flexible nature of the review process, not all reviews will go through all phases and may actually skip certain phases. All reviews begin with the Identification/Investigation Phase. The potential review candidates then go through the Internal Notification Phase. The approved review candidates then go through the Customer Notification Phase. During the Customer Notification Phase, some audits may be dropped, while most others will transition either to the Audit Phase (an actual audit - either a self audit or an audit conducted by an independent auditor) or jump directly to the Settlement Phase. Each of these phases is described below in more detail.

Phase one – identification/investigation

The Director of License Management will review all non-compliance leads and assign those leads to be actively investigated based on available resources and the nature of the leads. Once an Audit Manager is assigned a customer compliance target to investigate, a case file is created and the investigation begins.

Using internal resources and external information, the Audit Manager compiles the information required to complete the Customer Review Packet. The packet contains four main analysis documents:

- **Target Analysis Form**: With three main sections that include purchase data, subjective indicators around asset management practices, and other external factors that may be known.
- **Account Manager Questionnaire**: Used to document issues from the perspective of the customer's Account Manager.
- **Purchase Reconciliation Form**: Used to summarize all internal customer purchase data that must be obtained from the Account Manager.
- **Contract Summary Form**: Used to identify potential compliance issues that are specific to that customer contract. It is to include any amendments to the standard contract.

Once the information is complete, the Audit Manager makes an audit recommendation to the Director of License Management. In most cases, identified compliance issues must exist in the analysis when an audit is recommended. Submitting this recommendation (via e-mail) as part of the completed Target Analysis Form in the Customer Review Packet is the final task of the Identification/Investigation phase. Typically, this phase should take no more than 2 weeks to complete.

Phase two – internal notification

The Target Analysis Form is reviewed for completeness by the Director of License Management. An internal e-mail signifying the intent to audit this targeted customer is sent to the Sales Management team for the customer account, as well as other company executives, for example, the VP of Business Operations, the EVP of WW Field Operations, the General Counsel, and the CFO. Provided no unexpected issues arise, the audit recommendation is approved. This portion of the internal notification phase takes approximately 2-4 days.

For those audit candidates where the recommendation is NOT to continue with an immediate audit, the target analysis is filed. The complete Customer Review Packet is stored in the Compliance Group department files. If a deferred audit is recommended, it is the Audit Manager's responsibility to set up a calendar reminder.

For those candidates where the recommendation is to proceed with an audit and the decision is made to engage an independent auditor, the Director of License Management must first contact the independent auditor to obtain in writing that there are no potential conflicts of interest between the candidate and the auditing firm. If any arise, the Director of License Management contacts an alternate auditing firm. Once a potential auditing firm has been identified and cleared of any conflicts of interest, the Internal Notification Phase is complete. Only in cases where there are conflicts of interest will this portion of the process take more than one week.

Once an audit has been approved, the Audit Manager is responsible for notifying each regional sales VP and the VP finance. This notification should include the customer name and type of audit, and should be sent via e-mail.

Phase three – customer notification

The Audit Manager begins this phase by completing the Customer Notification Letter. This includes working with the sales team to identify the appropriate customer contact if this information is not already included in the Customer Review Packet. If the sales team does not have an appropriate contact, then contact information is pulled from Hoovers. In many cases it may take multiple customer contacts before the appropriate contact is identified, which may delay the timing of the actual customer notification. The Audit Manager will contact the customer via telephone to inform them of the desired audit and to expect the written notification. The notification letter, an official letterhead, is then e-mailed to the customer. If the customer has not responded within a week, the Audit Manager follows up the e-mail notification with telephone contacts.

Based on the customer response, the Audit Manager may just clarify the notification contents and proceed to an onsite audit. Typically there is an escalation process that requires the License Management Services (LMS) management team to become involved in the notification. At this stage, the customer may agree to an audit, or propose either a self-audit or a settlement offer. This first round of customer notification escalation should take no more than 1-2 weeks.

If an audit date is not agreed to within the initial 1-2 week notification period, the case will be escalated to the Director of License Management, who sends out an internal notification email to the VP of Business Operations, the General Counsel, and the EVP of WW Field Operations. Additional customer meetings are held and, within the following 1-2 weeks, another determination is made as to how to proceed: audit, self-audit, settlement or drop the case. (At this stage, a self-audit is rarely a preferred option due to the customer's resistance and the low likelihood of an accurate outcome).

In those cases where little progress is made towards reaching an audit agreement, the LMS management may elect to terminate the audit process. As with all audit terminations, all customer correspondence and background information is filed in the case file. The Director of License Management sends out an internal notification email to the VP of Business Operations, the General Counsel, and the Sales Management team for the customer account.

Phase four – audit

The Audit Phase can take one of two forms: an on-site audit or a customer self-audit. Either format has the same goal - to collect enough data regarding what product is installed and how it is managed to enable the software company to make an informed decision as to the extent to which the customer may or may not be in compliance with their license agreement.

Both versions follow the same high-level approach, and both may take up to 6-10 weeks to complete. The key difference is in who performs certain audit tasks.

On-Site Audit—once the customer has agreed to the audit, the Audit Manager or the independent auditing firm may proceed with the review. The auditor then contacts the customer to schedule an opening meeting to introduce the team and review process, establish review objectives and scope, and review the customer's contractual responsibilities. This should take no more than 2-3 weeks to accomplish. On a high level, the objectives of each review will include:

- Educating the customer on their obligations and responsibilities under the contract. This will include highlighting those issues that have been identified in the Customer Review Packet and addressing specific licensing questions posed by the customer.
- Reviewing the customer's SAM procedures and providing recommendations when needed.
- Obtaining and analyzing the customer's purchase and license usage data.

The scope of the review is verified with the customer and all parent and subsidiary companies under the contract (that are within scope) are documented with how they relate to the IT environment being tested. The process for determining the customer's license usage has two main parts—gathering customer technical data and reconciling the customer's purchases:

1. Collect information about the customer's IT environment and how the software company's products are deployed within it.
2. Obtain certification on the completeness of the IT environment being tested as documented from the IT Director or above.
3. Review the customer's Software Policy (if applicable) and, if not applicable, emphasize the relevance of having one.
4. If the customer utilizes a third-party SAM application within their IT environment, review the results of any reporting they can provide. This can provide an additional benchmark for the customer's license usage. Unless the customer's results can be validated completely, continue with the established routine process.
5. Review the discovery tool and its functions with the customer. Have them run the tool and retrieve the data, providing you with the data in an acceptable format and through an acceptable medium.

6. Analyze data and review with the customer, asking appropriate questions that will assist both parties in coming to an acceptable count of product licenses currently being used/deployed.
7. Meet with the customer purchasing representative and have them provide you with all purchasing data they have that falls within the scope of the review.
8. Reconcile the software company's purchase data with what the customer provided, noting variances and reasons.
9. Input both the technical data and the purchasing data into a findings sheet that compares the customer's usage with their purchases and identifies any variances.

The customer review will end with a closing meeting where all relevant participants in the review are required attendees. The review facts and findings will be presented and the customer will sign off on the findings sheet that the findings are accurate and they are in agreement. If the findings indicate the customer must make a purchase, then the customer will also agree to make the purchase. This may also complete the settlement phase of the audit process.

The software company will monitor incoming orders to verify the receipt of any required purchase order as per the review findings. Within 2-3 days following the audit, the independent auditor provides verbal preliminary feedback to the Audit Manager. The actual written Audit Report is sent to the Audit Manager within 10 days from the end of the audit.

The Audit Report is reviewed by the LMS management team to determine if the audit is complete and if the customer appears to be compliant. This review can take 2-3 days. The next step depends on the customer:

- If the customer appears compliant, then the audit is closed. The Audit Manager files all case documentation: the Customer Review Packet, the Customer Notification Letter, the Audit Report, and any other customer correspondence, including all copies of purchase data. The Director of License Management sends an internal notification email to the VP of Business Operations, the General Counsel, the EVP of WW Field Operations, and the Sales Management team for the customer account detailing the results of the audit.
- If the customer appears NOT to be compliant, then the audit proceeds to the settlement phase.

If needed, further review may be determined to be necessary at the discretion of the LMS management team. At some point, the audit will be determined to be complete, or as complete as it ever will be and a decision will be made to proceed to the settlement phase or to close the audit.

Customer Self-Audit—Once a self-audit has been agreed to by both parties, the customer must identify an employee to act as the Customer's Audit Coordinator. The Audit Manager schedules the audit and e-mails a self-audit package to the Customer's Audit Coordinator. An opening meeting is scheduled with the customer's audit coordinator to review the process, establish the review objectives and scope, review the customer's contractual responsibilities and answer any customer questions about the Self-Audit Package. The customer then agrees to a timeframe to complete the gathering and analysis of data to conclude the review. This portion of the Self-Audit process may take between 2-4 weeks, depending upon the knowledge and expertise of the Customer's Audit Coordinator, the overall level of cooperation and the institutional knowledge of their company's compliance practices.

The actual Self-Audit then takes place. The Customer Audit Coordinator completes the relevant portions of the Self-Audit Package and e-mails it back to the Audit Manager for review.

The Self-Audit Package is first reviewed by the Audit Manager to determine if the Self-Audit is complete. If it is, then it is evaluated to determine if the customer appears to be compliant. These should take 2-3 days. The next step depends on the customer:

- If the audit is complete AND the customer appears compliant, then the audit is closed. The Audit Manager files all case documentation: the Target Analysis Form, the Customer Notification Letter, the work, the Self-Audit Package, and any other customer correspondence. The Senior Director of Anti-Piracy sends the internal notification email is to the VP of Business Operations, the General Counsel, the EVP of WW Field Operations, and the Sales Management team for the customer account.
- If the audit is complete AND the customer appears to NOT be compliant, then the audit proceeds to the settlement phase.
- If the audit is NOT complete, then a follow-on Self-Audit must take place.

Before a follow-on Self-Audit takes place, the Director of License Management sends out an internal notification email to the VP of Business Operations, the General Counsel, the EVP of WW Field Operations, and the Sales Management team for the customer account.

The Audit Manager then contacts the Customer's Audit Coordinator to explain the necessity for a follow-on Self-Audit. This should take no more than 2 weeks to set up.

The follow-on Self-Audit may take between 1-3 days, depending on the nature of the additional information being collected.

The Customer Audit Coordinator obtains the additional information to complete the Self-Audit Package and e-mails it back to the Audit Manager.

The Self-Audit Package is again reviewed by the Audit Manager to determine if the audit is complete. If it is, then it is evaluated to determine if the customer appears to be compliant. This review should take 1-2 days. If the follow-on Self-Audit is still not complete, additional Self-Audits are not undertaken. Instead, if additional information is still needed, a full onsite audit is performed.

Phase five – settlement

Using the information collected during the audit, the Audit Manager creates/reviews the Customer Review Findings Sheet. The findings sheet covers any costs/fees to be paid, specifies the quantities of software licenses the customer owns, and compares what they own to what they are using, noting any license variances that they will need to purchase. All findings are then finalized and sent for LMS management team approval. This should take 1-3 days.

The findings are reviewed and approved by the Director of License Management and then sent to the VP of Business Operations and the Sales Management team for the customer account for their review. Any issues are resolved and the final proposal is ready to be presented to the customer within 5 days.

The Audit Manager presents the Customer Review Findings sheet to the customer. If the customer does not accept the terms within a week, the settlement is escalated to the Director of License Management. If the settlement is still not resolved after an additional 2-3 weeks, it is then escalated to the General Counsel, the VP of Business Operations and the EVP of WW Field Operations. If no settlement is reached after an additional 1-2 weeks, a decision must be made on whether to proceed with litigation or to drop the case.

Throughout the settlement process, once the customer has signed and sent back the original Customer Review Findings Sheet, which is legally binding, the audit will be considered closed. The originals are filed in the case file, and the software company will monitor incoming orders to verify the receipt of any required purchase order as per the review findings. Any corresponding purchase orders or settlement payments are booked and should be received within 4 weeks. All correspondence and audit materials are filed in the case file and the Director of License Management sends out an internal notification email to the VP of Business Operations, the General Counsel, the EVP of WW Field Operations, and the Sales Management team for the customer account, notifying them of the completion of the audit process.

Frequently asked questions

What is the License Management Services Program?

The purpose of the **License Management Services (LMS)** program is to assist customers in obtaining the goal of legal licensing throughout their enterprise IT environment. While we are concerned about contract compliance, this will be an educational process that will provide customers with the ability to assess themselves on an ongoing basis and provide them a methodology for maintaining contract compliance going forward. Customers will also establish a baseline for license ownership and usage that will allow them to look back to that point to know what products are owned and deployed in their environment.

The LMS Program is a global program that encompasses all Enterprise and Master License customers.

Who will perform the work?

The review will be conducted by members of the LMS team of Business Objects. It is possible that involvement by a third-party organization will be utilized for on-site work, but the review would still be overseen by internal team members.

Who will be involved from my organization?

Because of the many components of most enterprise customers' IT environments, and the breadth of any compliance review, involvement in the review may require input from any of the following: CIO, IT director(s), Business Unit IT Managers, Network/Systems Administrators, Purchasing Manager, Contract Administrator, and employee users of products.

What will be reviewed?

The LMS team will seek to determine your compliance with the terms of your contract and to understand your internal controls over SAM as it relates to the purchase/usage of software. For a more detailed overview of the process, please refer to the above process narrative.

How long does a typical review take? Since all organizations are different, the amount of time a review will take depends on many things. The size of the organization; the complexity of their IT environment and the deployment within that environment; the availability and cooperation level of key players; the on-site versus remote approach; these all play into the length of the review.

Most on-site reviews will not take more than 5 business days to complete, but may last longer or even significantly shorter. The length a remote review can take is difficult to determine, due to variances in time between correspondences.

It should also be noted, that from the time of notification to the customer until the final closure of the review, the process may take from 6-10 weeks.

What can I do to prepare once I'm notified of an upcoming review?

You can prepare by collecting as much information as possible prior to the review, including purchasing data, usage data, IT environment information, etc.

You can also contact the software company or the independent auditor when you have questions, so as to mitigate as many issues as possible prior to the review.

What if I am not legally licensed? Are there penalties for non-compliance?

The contract states:

Section 9.8: If, as a result of Licensor's audit, it is determined that Licensee owes Licensor additional fees, then Licensee shall bear the reasonable cost of Licensor's audit and pay all past-due fees in accordance with the terms of this Agreement.

If the review shows that you are not in compliance with your contract, the software company asks that you purchase the required number of licenses shown as the variance on the findings sheet and all associated Maintenance fees back to the last co-term date or a reasonable alternative date.

What benefits can my organization receive from a compliance review?

The License Compliance Program is designed to be an educational experience for the customer. The review process can provide a forum where product licensing questions can be addressed and SAM principles and best practices will be reviewed. It can also provide an alternative feedback channel for the customer.

Because of this process, you will have better insight into your usage of software assets. In today's Sarbanes-Oxley environment, this kind of information and the internal controls around it can be immensely beneficial. The process will also help IT management establish a pattern of software legitimacy within the organization as a whole.

How can I know that results of the review are accurate?

The compliance review process is designed to engage the customer in all aspects. From the outset, the customer is an integral part of the review process. All aspects of the review will involve someone from the customer's organization and be as transparent as possible. All license usage data will be drawn directly from the customer's IT environment as well.

At the conclusion of the review, the customer will recognize the accuracy of the results because they will see how those results were arrived at, having been engaged throughout the entire process.

How will results be communicated?

During the closing meeting, the final results of the review will be presented to and discussed with the customer.

The results would be sent to the customer prior to the closing conference call of a remotely conducted review or self-audit.

Summary

You have learned various steps to take after the audit letter arrives to disseminate, cooperate, aggregate and mitigate for current and future audits. You have also learned about the vendor and auditors license compliance review process and how they determine to move forward with an audit or not.

The early steps for responding to an audit demand need to be taken very quickly, and in many cases simultaneously. The quicker wheels are set in motion, the more prepared your company will be to effect a positive outcome.

Audit demand letters usually require a response within 30 days. The initial response should come from your company's legal department, your company appointed SAM audit response contact, or vendor management. It is usually a phone call or email to the designated contact to acknowledge receipt of the demand. Then legal or company appointed SAM audit response contact or vendor management will prepare a follow-up response to confirm receipt of the audit demand, review any initial agreements made during the first conversation, and nearly always to request more time to prepare for the audit.

If your enterprise has an ITAM program in place and a complementary SAM program and **central asset repository (CAR)**, the ITAM and SAM teams should use it within a couple of days of receiving the demand letter to determine quickly what specified software is installed and what software is in use, where, and by whom. Although not as accurate as a physical self-audit (automated systems are only as good as the input controlled by their administrators), a quick SAM audit will help the legal team devise an early response to the audit demand.

The software audit team should include the following:

- **Senior management**: For important decisions, either the enterprise leader (CEO, president, and so on.) or a designated member from senior management should be directly involved in the audit. Remember, the potential risks and costs could be very high depending on the size of an organization and its readiness.
- **Legal**: Expert legal counsel is essential in the event of an audit, and management should make sure that at least one member of the legal team—internal or external—has some experience with software audits.
- **SAM/IT/Application Owner**: No lawyer or senior manager can be expected to have a solid grasp of an enterprise's current IT estate, or future IT needs. The CIO and others in an IT department certainly should, and either an internal or external IT licensing expert with experience in navigating the nuances of a software audit is essential. Their expertise is needed not only during the self-audit and reporting processes, but especially during resolution strategy and negotiations. This is where an IT licensing expert is most likely to have valuable historical vendor knowledge and experience in brokering creative compromises and solutions that can save an organization thousands, or even millions, of dollars.
- **Finance/Procurement/VMO**: The CFO or someone close to them should be directly involved, along with representatives from accounting and purchasing to make sure the self-audit and report are accurate.

In descending order of preference, the four types of software audits are:

- **Self-audits**: Either a software vendor or a trade association acting on behalf of the vendor will request that an organization conduct an internal audit and report the results. By far the most favorable option, self-audits give an enterprise more flexibility in terms of timing and resource allocation, and they remain in control of the accuracy of the final report/summary. If another type of audit is demanded, most enterprises will counter with an offer to conduct a self-audit instead. Regardless of what type of audit is finally conducted, smart enterprises always conduct a self-audit - automated and/or physical - in advance to give themselves a complete picture of the facts pertaining to the audit demands, to help them devise the best response strategy, and to avoid ugly surprises.

- **Independent audits**: Although many software licenses include the vendor's right to request an independent audit, they should be avoided if possible. Independent audits by third-party accounting firms can be costly and time-consuming, and the enterprise has little or no influence over who performs the audit, how long it will take, or the specific items to be scrutinized. Typically, the vendor bears the cost of the audit unless a licensing discrepancy of more than X percent—usually five percent—is found. In that case, the organization not only pays for the audit, but the vendor can usually dictate the price of any additional software needed to become compliant. Penalties are at the discretion of the vendor. The main advantage of this type of audit is the ethical obligation of the auditor to act independently, unlike the next two options.

- **SAM engagements**: Microsoft is especially fond of this approach, in which the vendor pays a third-party to conduct an audit and report back to the vendor, normally using the targets' installed SAM system. Although typically less costly than self-audits or independent audits, SAM engagements are less likely to require the independence of the auditor from the vendor. On the plus side, vendors who request SAM engagements are usually only interested in full compensation for your actual software usage, and will often dispense with compliance penalties if the organization agrees to true-up and remain in compliance moving forward.

- **Vendor audits**: The least impartial and most intrusive form of audit, vendor-staffed inspections mean granting vendor employees access to your computer network so that they can verify an organization's compliance status. Software publishers often have a legal right to demand a vendor-staffed audit, but it is never wise to agree to one before attempting to negotiate an alternative.

The largest task of the audit response team is to conduct a thorough physical audit of all active, inactive, stored, and remote hardware—servers, laptops, repositories, and backup systems—and the software products mentioned in the demand letter. Undertaken as quickly as possible to enable the best response strategy, the physical audit validates and/or corrects the automated SAM inventory, if one was conducted. Very often, the validity of discovery tools such as a SAM program is in question, so a complete physical audit is beneficial and essential.

During the physical self-audit, the SAM audit response team gathers original copies of all media, certificates of authenticity, and proofs of purchase (current RFPs, POs, invoices, and receipts). An organization should store the originals in an offsite repository, but copies must be kept in the ITAM-SAM central repository. Photocopies of original owner documentation are accepted as valid proof of ownership for audits and usage.

Ownership documentation includes:

- Contracts
- End user license agreements
- Purchase invoices
- Certificates of authenticity
- Bills of lading
- Software boxes (flattened and placed in a labeled storage container)

Anyone who has conducted a physical self-audit knows that maintaining an inventory of all software licensed to the enterprise in a central asset repository makes it much easier to provide proof of ownership for a complete list of assets in the company's environment. An automated discovery system ensures the updating of inventory data when new software enters the system. It also allows the company to secure the original and backup copies as proof of ownership documents and installation media very quickly and efficiently.

Caution

During an automated or physical software audit, it is not unusual for members of the IT department to discover a number of non-compliance situations. Unfortunately, it is human nature to attempt to remove installed software from computers on the spot to avoid penalties, but this can be traced easily by independent auditors. One instance of removed software will make outside auditors suspicious, opening the door to a broadening of the audit parameters and more vigilant inspection. Another imprudent reaction to attempt compliance after an audit has been demanded is to purchase more software. Only software purchased before the date of the demand letter is relevant, so this ploy is also imprudent. Management should make it clear in advance that these reactions are not acceptable.

The goal of performing a software license review is to help ensure software usage compliance. It will allow you to understand your current licensing position as well as help you detect areas of inconsistent version installments that can be reduced to lower IT support costs. The reconciliation of license entitlements to license deployment will allow you to focus on purchasing software you need while limiting purchases for software no longer in use.

The first initial steps in responding to an audit demand should be completed as quickly as possible, ideally ahead of the timeframe specified in the demand letter. This timeframe is typically 30 days, but can be as little as one week. This is why the Legal team or SAM Audit Response contact almost always asks for more time. An optimal response strategy cannot be formulated until the organization has completed the physical self-audit and validation process, which inform the enterprise of their compliance status, an estimate of the potential financial cost at stake, and their negotiating leverage.

Lawyers and IT professionals familiar with software resolution frameworks must work closely together to determine the best response strategy. Legal counsel will focus primarily on the parameters and processes of the audit, the type of audit, the legal rights of the enterprise within the context of the software license terms and conditions, and negotiation/litigation options that range from switching to a different software to evaluating the probability of success based on the facts and a host of relevant legal considerations.

IT professionals with software audit resolution experience will leverage their intimate knowledge of software vendor tendencies and focus more on practical compromise solutions that can reduce potential fines and software costs dramatically.

Legal and the IT/SAM team will arrive at a strategy that combines cooperation, thorough preparation, and negotiation based on:

- The legal facts
- Resolution framework options
- IT-based conciliation/optimization solutions
- The best long-term interests of both the enterprise and the software vendor

Your organization's preparation and cooperation pays off when it comes to negotiating the cost of potential fines and legal fees. A combination of your legal department's expertise and organization's cooperation, typically with your IT department, throughout the audit process typically pays off with lower fines and legal fees than those originally indicated in the demand letter, or in the first pass at a settlement. The terms negotiated should include limitations on settlement publicity, providing affidavits from company officers rather than future audits, and so on.

The proactive approach now

When you consider all that is at stake for your company, are you sure you want to wait for an audit demand letter to arrive before deciding how your company will respond? When that happens, you have limited time and resources to correct or at least minimize your company's liability. Isn't it better to establish your plan now and prepare for the inevitable audit? Is your company doing whatever it takes to minimize your non-compliance threat? If not, I suggest you consider hiring a certified SAM consultant to help develop your policies, processes, and procedures. Then conduct a test audit and make any changes required. That way, when your company receives a demand letter, there is a response plan in place and your data repository gives you an accurate idea of your risk of exposure. The added bonus is that senior management knows it can react quickly, effectively, and confidently.

In addition, at a minimum, two programs will help an enterprise maintain compliance while facilitating optimal use and cost of software while protecting against potential disasters.

ITAM/SAM: as a part of ITAM, SAM encompasses the infrastructure and processes necessary to effectively manage, control and track software assets through all stages of their lifecycle.

Successful implementation of a SAM program will:

- Reduce audit exposure & potential financial risk to the enterprise
- Reduce security risks from unauthorized software within the environment
- Reduce software costs while improving the budgeting process and financial controls

Software Disaster Recovery Planning: The objective of a software disaster recovery plan is to ensure that an enterprise can recover its inventory data, installation media, and proof of ownership documents in the event of a crisis. This happens to be exactly what is needed in the case of an audit. Similarly, the steps needed to keep a disaster recovery plan up to date also apply to ensuring that the information needed during an audit remains current. Finally, the same thinking that goes into recovering from disasters such as fire and floods also applies to surviving the perils of a software audit. The money saved in the event of disaster is more than enough to justify the cost of a software disaster recovery program; the fact that it also helps organizations survive a software audit doubles the value. With thoughtful planning a company can not only recover from a disaster, it can also have a ready, effective response to a demand letter that ensures the company survives an audit with minimal impact.

The next chapter focuses on ITAM/SAM tools, ITAM/SAM tools strategy, what you should look for in an ITAM/SAM tool and how to determine what your requirements should be.

ITAM Tools – What Should You Look For?

6

Few areas affect your enterprise to the extent that technology does. It affects your budget, your spending, your results, your capabilities, your people, your processes and—ultimately your success. The whole concept behind applying technologies to business intelligence and processes is to ensure that you work smarter, not harder, which in turn should lead to improved results.

The choice of technology is one of the more difficult aspects of **Information Technology Asset Management (ITAM)** and **Software Asset Management (SAM)**. There are tools that can do ITAM well but not SAM. There are tools that do SAM well, but don't do overall ITAM well, because they are not robust enough to handle **Hardware Asset Management (HAM)**. There are tools that state they can do it all.

Using today's technology, an intelligent asset (such as a laptop, mobile device, server, or VM) reports the manufacturer, make, model, and serial number. The position on the network is also known. Reports include the installed processor(s), software, memory, drives, card(s), and potentially connected peripherals. So *why is ITAM/SAM so hard to do and the choice of tool so critical?* The intelligent asset does not know the following:

- *What cost center to report?*
- *Who is using the technology?*
- *Who is responsible for the asset?*
- *Where it is located?*
- *How to report data to match the PO or license?*
- *How much it is costing your organization?*

It also cannot tell you anything once it has been disconnected from the network and placed under a desk or in a closet—yet that's precisely the point in the life cycle of an asset that yields the highest value. Automation that supports process as well as data collection is essential to value delivery. For instance, an ITAM/SAM tool that supports workflow can be designed to automatically open a request ticket to pick up the assets when an employee is either moving to a different location or exiting an organization. The tool cannot force the HR resource to trigger the workflow or the former employee's manager to cooperate by relinquishing the assets, but that is where process and awareness programs increase the success of the product and processes.

An IT asset is dynamic in nature; therefore, it is imperative that your organization can keep up with the pace. As we covered in `Chapter 2`, *ITAM Strategy and Plan*, create a strategic plan for managing your IT assets, then identify the tools that will best support your plan, and most importantly, define all of the processes to support the infrastructure identified. Unfortunately, there is no magic product that can fix your company's ITAM pitfalls, and processes do not change overnight. However, there are many tools that can help your organization achieve its asset management goals. This chapter will help you tailor a tool strategy and plan, for your specific organization, how to determine your tool's current and future needs, and what questions you need to ask yourself when evaluating tools before purchase.

Determining your current needs and future needs

ITAM is the proactive process of tracking and analyzing the technical and financial information of an organization's hardware and software. This process spans the life cycle of hardware and software assets from the moment the asset is requisitioned through its procurement, receipt, deployment, maintenance, and retirement.

To understand your current ITAM or SAM situation, and determine cost-effective best practice processes and automated ITAM/SAM systems that help you meet the goals of reduced waste, improved profitability, and achieving software license compliance and audit readiness (as we covered in `Chapter 2`, *ITAM Strategy and Plan*), you will need to do the following:

1. Conduct an assessment of your current organization's situation and practices, including the following:

   - Organization and roles, including structure, skills, and staffing levels
   - Current processes for software contracts, procurement, billing, payment, and asset tracking
   - Current and planned ITAM/SAM technologies that support billing and payment, asset discovery, tracking, and disposition
   - Current and planned projects that could affect your ITAM initiative

2. Deliver an assessment report which will include the following:

   - SWOT analysis covering strengths, weaknesses, opportunities, and threats, with the results including short-term actions and long-range planning recommendations
   - Gap analysis detailing gaps between current practices and best practices
   - Best practice recommendations to improve ITAM and SAM capabilities and audit readiness
   - Tactical systems roadmap for ongoing improvements and to increase the effectiveness of existing systems while developing or re-designing processes
   - Data dictionary including source and data elements for integration and standardization
   - Automation customization findings—implementing changes inspired by the analysis

3. Deliver a roadmap and budget estimates for implementing the recommendations to achieve:

- Proactive asset management
- Software contract/license compliance
- Reduced business and legal risk
- Improved controls and accurate reporting on IT assets, contracts, licenses, and usage
- Cost savings through waste elimination and market-price alignments
- Audit readiness
- Cost savings based on opportunities to align contract price with market price

Questions to think about when defining your asset life cycle:

- *How do we acquire our assets?*
- *How do we deploy or install our assets?*
- *What happens when an asset moves?*
- *What happens when an asset is repaired?*
- *What happens when an asset is retired or disposed of?*
- *Do we know what applications we are licensed for?*
- *Are we monitoring our license purchases?*
- *Do we know what our license terms are?*
- *Do we reharvest/reuse software licenses?*

The answers to these questions will help you to start thinking and forming your requirements and needs.

Each of these pieces should be thought about not just in terms of the physical asset, but the financial aspects related to that asset as well. For example, when an asset is moved, there is more than just the physical move to consider. There are costs involved, which can vary from the technician sent to complete the move, network drops, and so on.

Here's another example—when an asset is retired, it is important to know if the asset was leased or purchased. A purchased asset is often tracked and depreciated by the accounting or financials department, so they will need to be notified to remove this asset from the books. By defining processes, your organization can move from asset tracking to asset management.

Questions to think about when defining automated processes and integrations are as follows:

- *Do we need to integrate our procurement vendors with the asset repository (ITAM tool)?*
- *Should we reconcile our physical inventory baseline with auto-discovery data?*
- *Do we need to integrate the asset repository with the service desk application/tool?*
- *Do we need to integrate with the fixed asset or other financial systems?*

An ideal goal of ITAM is to achieve a level of automation that will lower your total cost of ownership of both your IT assets and the repositories that manage and utilize them. An important thing to remember is that achieving integration is not just moving data from one system to another. Rather, it is the bi-directional movement of data between two systems—working together will maximize the benefits of both systems. It is also important to determine the primary recording system, sometimes called as **system of record** (**SOR**) for particular data elements in order to not have core elements overwritten by a less trusted source.

A **data dictionary** is a repository for descriptions of data types or object types. Data dictionaries are used to store definitions of, for example, item types and their attributes. This allows users to see what item types have been defined and what their uses are:

- They can be consulted to understand *where a data item fits in the structure, what values it may contain*, and basically, *what the data item means in real-world terms*
- A data dictionary holds the following information as follows:
  - Consistency between data items across different tables
  - Information about the stored data
  - Details of the data's meaning
  - Origin, usage, and format

This master list will enable the correct population of your central asset repository (CAR/ITAM tool) with the best possible accuracy and standardization. Data sources can come from various spreadsheets, access databases, and other systems.

System integrations are a critical way to maximize your ITAM repository. These integrations can be challenging from a technical and political standpoint.

What to look for when selecting a tool?

There are many choices for ITAM and SAM tools, so you really need to plan in advance what you need the tool to do for your organization and users. You need to have a holistic approach. The tool should be able to manage financial, contractual, and physical data, integrate with adjacent IT management tools and business systems, provide out-of-the box best practice functionality, and support the implementation and automation of processes.

If you are selecting an ITAM/SAM tool for your organization for the first time, it is important to keep certain things in mind so that you get the right tool to meet your specific business requirements.

Asset management versus asset tracking

Tracking is not ITAM. While asset tracking and asset management exhibit similar functions, there are significant differences between the two.

Asset tracking: Deals with the physical characteristics of hardware and software in support of planning, deployment, operation, support, service, and installation/use data.

Asset management: Deals with the fiscal (financial and/or contract) details of hardware and software as required for financial management, risk management, contract management, vendor management, and ownership data. Asset tracking is a prerequisite.

Asset tracking systems manage IT assets from a physical perspective, capturing information such as CPU type and speed, memory, installed software, components, and operating system. This allows organizations to know what they have, where is it, and how it is configured. Sophisticated tracking systems take this one step further and keep a complete history of all changes to the asset. Companies like to think that the discovery tool they sometimes own is an asset tracking / asset management tool. That is 100% false. It is only one piece of the puzzle. While discovery tools can report the application installations found, they cannot tell you if the software is licensed. Obtaining the relationship between the installation and the license is crucial to achieving software asset management.

ITAM systems can also track the physical components of the assets; in addition, allow you to know where the asset is, and who the asset has been assigned to. In fact, to accomplish this, data is often taken directly from asset-tracking systems and integrated with asset management systems. The similarities end here though, as asset management systems go beyond tracking the physical components of assets, and provide the ability to manage the non-physical components of assets: for example, user and owner information, fiscal and contractual aspects of assets, such as warranty information, leasing and maintenance contracts, software licensing, original purchase cost, and current value. Often, these non-physical components of assets represent the greatest percent of the total cost of ownership.

It is critical that ITAM/SAM systems are integrated with other existing systems in addition to asset tracking systems. These systems usually include procurement, financial, enterprise architecture, human resources, contract management, change management, and help desk systems. Without such integration, ITAM/SAM systems quickly become cumbersome and out of date as demographic and component data soon becomes inaccurate and produces substantial increases in labor costs, unnecessary equipment losses, and duplicate purchases of IT assets (hardware and software).

An ideal asset management solution

An ideal asset management solution transparently takes *snapshots* of hardware and software assets on a regular basis and stores this asset information in a **central asset repository (CAR)**. This repository should include an accurate, up-to-the-minute view and a historical perspective of IT assets, enabling organizations to determine what their assets look like today, as well as the speed and direction of their change.

Your ideal asset management solution should also provide a superior effort-to-value ratio. Namely, minimal effort results in tremendous value. To accomplish this, the ideal solution should automatically generate pointed analyses that transform raw data into pertinent information. This information can be used to facilitate decision-making for each department, including purchasing, IT, security, operations, and finance. The end result is cost savings and productivity enhancements throughout the organization:

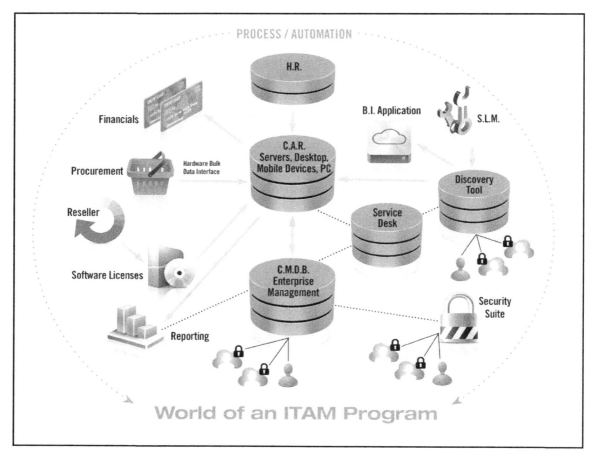

ITAM bridges the gap between operational and financial systems to enable organizations to save money, make money, and stay in compliance

Asset management process considerations

It is critical to incorporate process flow into the ITAM tool as well. Far too often, ITAM/SAM tools are expected to magically fix a process problem. It is important to understand that all any software application does is automate a series of processes. If the right processes are not in place within the organization and effectively integrated into the selected software application, then the risk of not realizing the full benefit and ROI or even outright project failure goes up significantly.

The following diagram illustrates the high-level overview processes for full enterprise life cycle of IT asset management:

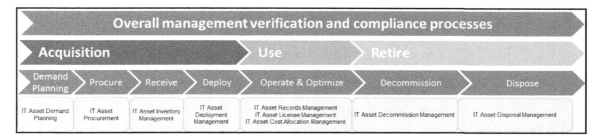

Common product/tool terminology

The common product/tool terminologies are as follows:

- **Discovery or auto-discovery**: The ability to find new, moved, or changed assets
- **Auditing**: Scanning an asset to record its attributes
- **Repository**: A dynamic database of IT assets (hardware and software) and their components and attributes
- **Software recognition**: *How software installed is recognized?*
- **Software reconciliation**: The ability to match up hardware to software installations to software purchase history
- **Contracts management**: The ability to manage, prioritize, and comply with contracts and agreements
- **Reporting**: The ability to share, collaborate, and act on asset data
- **Workflow and automation**: The ability to automate processes
- **Systems management**: To deliver changes, maintenance, or new deployments

Determine products, services, and features needed, such as the following:

- Cloud or web-based
- Discovery:
    - Scans for hardware and software on those assets that are on your network
- Asset management, software management, and contract management:
    - *Do you want one ITAM tool that includes all these functions/modules,* or *do you want a tool that specializes only in asset management?*
- Native apps for iOS, Android, and Windows devices:
    - Allows easy access by users after hours and offsite
- Asset auditing function:
    - Allows timeframes setup, limits information seen when performing an audit, and allows changes for unrecorded and missing assets
- Asset check in/check out:
    - Receiving and loaning assets, and multi-item check-in and checkout options
- Built in asset tag/barcode creation:
    - System can create asset tags and barcodes for each asset
- Disposed/recovery asset function:
    - Look for the ITAM tool to have a recover option that reactivates the old asset number/tag. Without the recover option, you will have to create a brand new asset and manually update the record with the old record's history, which may or may not be available anymore.
- Automated emails/in-app notifications/alerts:
    - Important: make sure mass alerts and notifications are also available
- Reports/ad hoc
- Security/access restrictions
- Available training
- Support/maintenance
- What systems need to be integrated? (HR, procurement, service desk, discovery)
- How will it be funded? Who will be paying for it?
- What are the pros and cons of in-house versus Saas?
- Which stakeholders will participate in related programs and activities?

Steps to consider while selecting an IT asset management tool for your business:

The steps are as follows:

1. Determine your ITAM/SAM program objectives and tools strategy:

   - *Where is your organization today? What are you looking to achieve? What are your goals?*
   - *What is in and out of scope?*
   - *Who are the top software publishers that we want to manage? Based on spend? Based on level of audit vendor conducts?*
   - *Are we focusing on high value assets only based on spend and risk?*
   - *What data do we need to manage? What systems do we need to integrate with?*
   - *How will we reconcile our data and manage accuracy?*
   - *Do we manage our IT assets though their entire life cycle? Do we have the correct processes in place? If so, are they followed?*
   - *Which teams will manage and support the ITAM program and tools?*

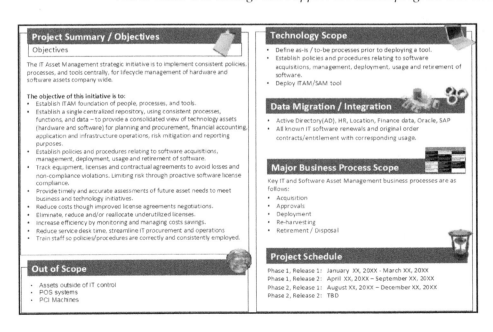

2. Know your business requirements as well as functional and technical requirements:

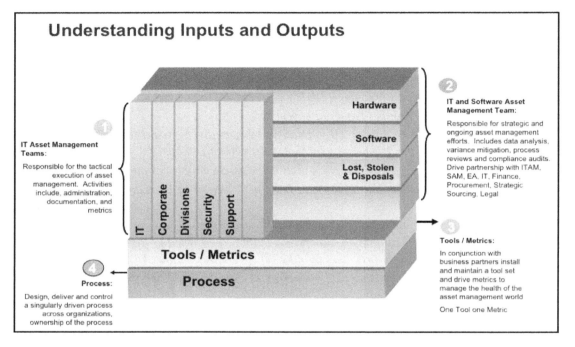

Understanding Inputs and Outputs

3. Research and look at multiple tool solution options online. Review customer feedback and ratings. You can also ask other individuals you have connections with at other companies what they use for an ITAM/SAM tool.

Tools that work for another organization, might not work for your organization.

Once you have a list, create a comparison matrix to compare the features and support options of the tools. Understand the usability and workflow features that the tool provides. At this early stage, hold off comparing the price. The following is an example of a high-level comparison matrix:

General Descriptors	Product A	Product B	Product C	Product D
Centralized Data Center Optimization	✓	✓	✓	✓
Change Control	✓	✓		
CMDB Data Quality	✓	✓	✓	✓
Business Service Management Integration	✓	✓		✓
Power Management		✓		
Standardization	✓	✓	✓	✓
Scalability and Ease of Use				
Proven scalability for large enterprises	✓	✓	✓	
Agentless ping sweeps/low impact scans	✓	✓	✓	
Browser-based interface	✓	✓		✓
Thick client-based interface	✓			✓
Data Center Recognition & Indexing Completeness				
Agent Free, Credential-based discovery	✓	✓	✓	✓
Agent based discovery	✓		✓	✓
Discover Applications	✓	✓	✓	✓
Discover Servers, Hardware, Printers, Applications, Storage, and Networking	✓	✓	✓	✓
Discover Web Services and dependencies	✓			✓
Discover J2EE applications	✓	✓	✓	✓
Discover databases	✓	✓		✓
Discover mainframes	✓	✓		
Discover virtual infrastructure	✓	✓	✓	
Discovery run scheduler	✓	✓	✓	✓
Discover Layer 2 topology	✓	✓		✓
Discover Layer 3 topology	✓	✓		
Discover VMWare	✓	✓	✓	
Discover Multi-platform	✓	✓		✓
Single-click leads to "failed discovery"	✓			
Platforms supported	AIX, HP/UX, Solaris, Linux, Windows, OS/2, and DOS	AIX, HP/UX, Solaris, Linux, Windows, OS/2, and DOS, Mac OS x, Tru64, NetBSD, Unix Ware, Open BSD, FreeBSD, IRIX	AIX, HP/UX, Solaris, Linux, Windows, OS/2, and DOS	AIX, HP/UX, Solaris, Linux, Windows, OS/2, and DOS
Analysis and Reporting				
Extensible data model	✓	✓		✓
Flexible recognition engine and scripting	✓	✓	✓	✓
Automated update service	✓	✓		✓
Integrated reporting and analysis	✓	✓	✓	
Critical dependency reporting/viewing	✓	✓		✓
Capable of configuration comparisons (points in time)	✓	✓		
Out-of-the-box normalized reports	✓	✓	✓	✓
Change tracking in real time	✓	✓		✓
Potential security threat viewing	✓	✓		✓
Full text search capability	✓	✓		✓
Graphical dashboard management	✓	✓		✓
Collaborative portal interface	✓			
Software Installations				
Identifies software installations	✓	✓	✓	✓
Identifies software installation version	✓	✓	✓	
Easily updates to add new software	✓	✓	✓	✓
Automatically discovers new software	✓	✓	✓	
Identifies authorized and unauthorized usage				
Identifies frequency of use	✓	✓	✓	✓
Integration				
Flexible CMDB and BSM tool integration	✓	✓		✓
Configurable Data Mapping	✓	✓		✓
Integration toolkits for custom applications	✓	✓	✓	✓
Comments				
Other points	Ease of use: Medium This product would really be more than you need.	Object-Mesh Database Search everything No artificial schema restrictions Extensible reasoning platform Monthly knowledge updates Automatic provenance Information stability Interactive analysis Focus – 100% focus on IT Discovery & Application Dependency maps		No archive feature for CIs not relevant to CMDB daily ops
Ease of use	medium	easy	easy	difficult
Ease of installation	easy	easy	easy	medium
Bandwith on Network	not bad	not bad	not bad	awful

High-level comparison matrix

4. ITAM/SAM tools are available at several price points. Vendors sometimes price their tool by number of devices or number of users who will be using the application. Determine if you want a one-time purchase or a monthly subscription. Be aware that some tools can have an additional cost for their vendor specific license modules if you need to manage Oracle, SAP, or Microsoft licenses, among others, and for integration connectors to other systems. In addition, there is the maintenance fee, which can be around 20% of the license cost and module/connector cost. For subscription based licenses the maintenance fee can be a flat fee.

5. Pick your top three or five ITAM/SAM tool choices and contact the vendor for a detailed demonstration of the product. Invite the demo key shareholders, sponsor, the folks that will be using the application, and some management from your organization. It is OK if you have to schedule multiple demo meetings.

6. Request customer referrals. This will allow you to ask existing customers the pros and cons they have experienced. One question I like to ask is this—if anything could be improved or done differently with the tool, *what would that be?* Also, if you know someone who is using the tool, you can ask them about the performance, usability, and scalability of the tool and where they purchased the tool.

7. Include the users and management of the ITAM/SAM tool in the evaluation process, and in key discussion meetings. They are the best people to decide whether the tool will fulfill all the requirements or not. User adoption of the tool is necessary to manage the assets properly, and it further helps in the reuse of the organization's software and hardware. It is also very important that management is involved and engaged. I have seen many ITAM/SAM programs and ITAM/SAM tools get derailed because management was not fully engaged or was distracted and decided the tool did not suit their needs, even though the ITAM/SAM tool did suit their needs. However, they delegated someone on their team to come to all meetings and demos. So, they did not see for themselves that the tool covered everything and more that they wanted. In short, make sure at a minimum that management attends one live demo and attends two key evaluation meetings, one at the beginning and one at the end of the process at least. This can make a big contribution to your success.

8. Usability. When you are close to making the final decision, remember to consider the tool that requires the least training and is the easiest to use. The software provider/vendor should provide training to your staff as well, so that they can operate the software easily. Also, require the software provider/vendor to provide super-care after the implementation of your ITAM/SAM tool before transferring you over to their customer support team.

9. Be prepared. There are sometimes additional costs that you will forget to prepare for your ITAM/SAM tool implementation once you have made your purchase. If you decide to have the tool managed in-house at your enterprise, do you have the infrastructure in stock, or will you have to purchase a physical server or VM. *Will you need to purchase a database license for SQL or Oracle, and so on?* Very important, budget for professional services and training. The cost for professional services can sometimes cost more than the tool itself. You will need the vendor to do the initial implementation setup and configuration. Than determine if you have existing staff who can proactively manage the system, are license **subject matter experts** (**SMEs**) for your managed software list (which are your high risk of audit, strategic software vendors, high spend applications). If not, have a line item in the budget for external help. You also cannot expect your team to be successful, if you have not provided the training they will need to manage all these new wonderful capabilities.

ITAM is more than hardware and IT

Every organization understands the vital importance of their IT systems, but very few pay attention to the successful implementation of ITAM/SAM tools, systems, and software programs.

The reasons for this alarming record of ITAM/SAM implementation failure range from lack of project ownership or management support to technical incompetence, lack of user input, lack of C-suite support, changing requirements or specifications, lack of resources, obsolescence, poor communication, insufficient training, and selection of the wrong ITAM system/tool, the list goes on. In fact, implementation failure occurs for all these reasons, and many more, but all of them are easily avoidable.

Strategic, tactical, and operational plagues

ITAM implementations can be challenging, and many initiatives fail. Issues that plague the implementations are typically categorized into three organizational levels—**strategic**, **tactical**, and **operational**.

By identifying these levels, specified issues can be placed within a framework for resolution, while keeping business and IT aligned:

Strategic	Tactical	Operational
➤ Undefined goals and objectives ➤ Lack of governance or ownership ➤ Lack of employee buy-in/resistance to change ➤ Lack of consensus ➤ Disconnect with the business strategy ➤ Extending ownership across departmental boundaries	➤ Lack of standards ➤ Weakness in process specification ➤ Weak or non-existent communication and education program ➤ Incorrect or no methodology ➤ Underestimated time to map and agree on processes ➤ No single, identifiable process owner	➤ Little to no tool support ➤ Lack of process visualization ➤ Perceived process design/execution gaps ➤ Misinterpretation of tool capabilities

It all starts with the comprehensive ITAM/SAM tools strategy that begins with an expert analysis of organizational needs and existing IT portfolios. Make allowances for likely future technology needs, and make certain all the C-suite and their direct reports are fully behind the project before proceeding. Finally, establish metrics to measure the success of the ITAM system/tool, and the implementation.

Once the planning is accomplished, guide your implementation every step of the way with the following:

- Realistic schedules, including logical phases
- Technology installation/supervision
- Employee and management training on-site
- ITAM system/tool monitoring to ascertain progress
- Optimization services to make necessary adjustments
- Ongoing audits and advice for further upgrades and improvements

Nothing is more important to your organization's ITAM/SAM program success along with solid processes than smooth, efficient IT systems.

Consider these requirements as a baseline for what your ITAM tool should and can address at a minimum:

Requirements Traceability Matrix (RTM)	
Sub Process (Level 2)	**Key Capabilities (Level 3 Activity/Use Case)**
Define program scope	No Level 3 Activity/Use Case required
Defining standards for technology	No Level 3 Activity/Use Case required
Define roles and responsibilities	No Level 3 Activity/Use Case required
Define tool requirements	Required tool infrastructure for non-production and production environments to include system monitoring, backups, redundancy, and disaster recovery.
Define tool requirements	Group licenses by internal application name
Define tool requirements	Show licenses by business owner
Define tool requirements	Show unused licenses that have already been purchased
Define tool requirements	Show non-compliance with over-extended licenses
Define tool requirements	How license by contracts
Define tool requirements	Software usage monitoring
Define tool requirements	Fields in which to track/enter contract number
Define tool requirements	Can track third-party relationships (VAR/reseller agreements)
Define tool requirements	License optimization to include both up- and downgrade licensing
Define tool requirements	Oracle-specific compliance and application visibility
Define tool requirements	Microsoft-specific compliance and application visibility
Define tool requirements	Adobe-specific compliance and application visibility
Define tool requirements	IBM-specific compliance and application visibility
Define tool requirements	VMware-specific compliance and application visibility
Define tool requirements	Software metering to report unused licenses already purchased, report over-extended licenses, and the historic tracking of licenses
Define tool requirements	System can provide the ability to track and allocate license costs to one or more cost centers
Define tool requirements	Has a field to track what divisions the software was acquired for, if specific to one or more, but not entire enterprise
Define tool requirements	Provides fields that can be used to describe what proprietary business systems/applications leverage the software licenses, and in what quantities, per app, and per environment
Define tool requirements	Provides fields to input and track the vendor contact information
Define tool requirements	Provides fields to track the budget years to allocate costs to
Define tool requirements	Provides fields to enter original Purchase Order Agreement numbers
Define tool requirements	Provides generic fields to enter comments or custom data
Define tool requirements	Grouping of licenses by application, business group, and internal applications
Define tool requirements	Grouping assets by application
Define tool requirements	Grouping assets by business owner

Requirements Traceability Matrix (RTM)

Requirements Traceability Matrix (RTM)	
Sub Process (Level 2)	**Key Capabilities (Level 3 Activity/Use Case)**
Define tool requirements	Add non-standard fields (for example, consoles, LOM, and peripherals)
Define tool requirements	Show top-down view of virtual assets (that is, show a VMware/OVM/Xen/ IBM VIO host and drill down to the virtual guests) Including:Operating system, Version, CPU/Memory, Network information & Disk layout
Define tool requirements	View of system details
Define tool requirements	Ability to track production systems versus non-production systems
Define tool requirements	Ability to track clusters/members and relationships
Define tool requirements	Ability to track hardware warranty data
Define tool requirements	Show assets' current status in the lifecycle (for example, active, decommissioned, repurposed, disposed)
Define tool requirements	Ability to be updated by role (for example, PMs can change an asset to active on go-live, ops can decom a system when requested)
Define tool requirements	Ability to group hardware and software assets by location/division
Define tool requirements	Ability to group operating system instances by application of the business group
Define tool requirements	Ability to group by data center
Define tool requirements	Ability to group by AD domain or OU membership
Define tool requirements	Audit management and reporting capability
Define tool requirements	Track/Alert on due dates for maintenance renewals, expiration dates, and so on
Define tool requirements	Tracks months to contract expiration
Define tool requirements	Tracks contract start date
Define tool requirements	Tracks contract end date
Define tool requirements	Has fields for tracking the internal manager/negotiator of the contract (and can preferably pull this data from the AD or GAL)
Define tool requirements	Has a field to track what divisions the software was acquired for, if specific to one or more, but not entire enterprise
Define tool requirements	Provides fields to track the contract dollar amounts
Define tool requirements	Provides the ability to embed links or attachments to original contracts, ELA's, and so on
Define tool requirements	Provides ability to classify and track license types (that is, perpetual versus SaaS)
Define tool requirements	Product provides the ability to track whether it is software licensing only, software and hardware licensing combined, or hardware only
Define integration requirements	Integration requirements to AD, will export user login ID and e-mail, as well as configure for SSO
Define integration requirements	Integration requirements for Oracle, will export from Oracle HR: employee first name, last name, e-mail, location, division, hire date, and term date

Requirements Traceability Matrix (RTM)

The importance of metrics – how to measure ITAM success

Metrics are a critical factor for ITAM success. You must measure your progress on a consistent basis. The ongoing measurement and comparison enables organizations to track progress and expose opportunities for improvement. In addition, metrics enable an organization to quantify and demonstrate value. You can set metrics by quantity, financial, compliance, quality, and duration.

Measurements and metrics

Focus on developing measures and metrics that serve core business objectives, support proactive risk management, and enable real assessment of the effectiveness and value of your ITAM program, processes, and tools.

The tables in each of the following sections are organized to enable the assignment of each selected measure or metric to an associated business driver. This is just an example:

EXAMPLE							
ITAM MEASURE OR METRIC	**BUSINESS DRIVERS**						
	COST MGT.	RISK MGT.	ROI, VALUE	LEGAL REQ.	POLICY REQ.	SAFETY	INTERNAL INFLUENCE
Software cost as a percentage of total company revenue	x		x				
Percentage of critical information assets or software residing on systems that are currently in compliance with the approved system architecture		x			x		x
Number of failed or ineffectual business unit responses to issues identified as control weaknesses that result from software non-compliance prevention analysis, investigations or other feedback		x					x
Number of nuisance alarms from corporate facilities monitored by Corporate Security	x	x				x	
Number of safety hazards proactively identified and eliminated annually		x		x	x	x	
SW compliance penalty avoidance	x	x	x		x		x
Re-use of reclaimed assets—both HW and SW to reduce current HW and SW overspend	x		x		x		x
Eliminate expenses for assets discovered to be no longer in possession, for example, HW maintenance, tax, insurance, and so on	x	x	x		x		
Vendor management - SW and contract negotiation on the customer's terms instead of the vendor's terms			x	x			

Assignment of metric to associated business driver

Actionable metrics

The following are the specific and repeatable tasks you can improve and tie to your organization's goals:

- **Trends**: External and internal risk factors
- **Change**: Relationship of ITAM program to an improved state of risk management

- **Project status**: Schedules, budget burn rates, results to plan, and so on
- **Value**: IT asset management, cycle times, cost management, ROI, and so on
- **Standards and benchmarks**: Use versus best practices and peers
- **ITAM's effectiveness**: Rated by customers
- **Accountability**: The diligence of line business unit managers to comply with ITAM/SAM policies and processes to protect against known risks and software noncompliance
- **Performance**: Measurement of staff, vendors, and so on
- **Business plan**: ITAM program performance against quantifiable objectives
- **Hygiene of the firm**: Business conduct, continuity, integrity, incident rates, and so on
- **Lessons-learned**: Case results, defect reduction, software reuse, audit after-action views
- **Business mission and strategy**: Contributions to the execution of the business mission and strategy

Here is an example:

Software Cost	Software cost per dollar of revenue is up past two quarters
Info Security	14% decrease Q2 versus Q1 in devices with appropriate patches installed and current
Business Conduct	Year-to-date investigative results indicate 20% increase in non-compliance with SAM polices
ITAM Audits	100% of all notable item-related audit findings have been successfully resolved
Business Continuity	17% of critical business processes do not have up-to-date and tested response plans

Summary

Do your homework before deciding to purchase an ITAM/SAM tool. Make sure to check if you already have an existing system/tool being used in your organization that could fulfill your needs. Don't get bogged down with features and customization possibilities. Don't pay for more than you need.

Overall, when selecting a tool to support your ITAM program you want to look for an asset repository that will centrally hold hardware, software, and usage information, have the ability to integrate to adjacent IT and business systems, and be able to both import and export data. In regard to SAM, you want to include being able to track software licenses, software contract agreements, downgrade and upgrade rights, ability to do software reconciliation, and provide license position reports, at a minimum.

I encourage you to think through your decision and include the main users of the tool and senior management in the evaluation process. I see it so often, where an ITAM tool implementation gets derailed because not everyone was on the same page, or did not truly understand the capabilities of the application. This derailment trickled down and set the customer's ITAM program back. Without efficient tools to help with automation, communication, reporting, and workflow to help folks to follow the process, processes start to fail.

This chapter has covered the correct questions to ask and answer and what you should look for when deciding on tools. In the next chapter, we will cover how change management increases ITAM program and project success.

7

Increasing ITAM Program and Project Success Rates using Change Management

When times get tough, the first things to go are the so called non-essential activities. It is human nature. Unfortunately, companies are not always good at identifying which activities these are, so end up making decisions that are often short-sighted. The IT industry has teetered on the brink of this particular dilemma on more than one occasion.

Back at the height of the dot.com boom, technology was king and IT development projects were rampant. Interestingly enough, during this same period, many of the Big 4 and other high profile development companies were focused as much on the field of change integration as on gaining efficiencies in the technology development process. We could build a solution, but the questions remained—*will what we build maximize value for the company*, and *will the new solution be adopted and used given the culture and structure of the target organization, or does that need to change?*

For reasons more to do with politics than good business sense, the two disciplines of change management and IT strategy and development evolved along their own paths for a number of years before finally starting to coalesce into a single approach. However, by then the world economy had started to turn and the momentum shifted to cost containment and maximizing development efficiencies, that is, how you get more out of less. Outsourcing became the new mantra, along with agile and speed to market. These are all very sensible approaches to the new economic environment, but at that point some of the valuable work conducted in the field of change management was shelved to focus too much on rapid development and good enough solutions.

Change management had built whole practices on topics such as the following:

- Conducting change readiness workshops
- Culture change assessments
- Envisioning change and designing the target environment
- Stakeholder management
- Managing communications
- Building efficient teams
- Skill transfer and performance-based training
- Establishing performance and reward systems
- Organizational change management

My contention is not that we need to go back to this world, but I hate to lose sight of the work. Thankfully, some of these topics have been absorbed into program and project management activities within the **Project Management Institute** (**PMI**), specifically in the areas of communications, team building, and stakeholder management, or have become product owner or scrum master activities in incremental and iterative development methodologies. So, it is not that everything has been lost, but there is a plethora of research in these areas that can help an **IT Asset Management** (**ITAM**) program and the projects within it be more successful.

In the *Converting Strategy into Action* course offered by Stanford University, they emphasize the importance of understanding the culture and the structure of a company as a critical input in moving ideas from a vision to a practical solution, and indicate that these same aspects have a direct bearing on the adoption and success rates of the endeavors, so I see the pendulum starting to swing back just a little.

At the same time, other more personal change management techniques, such as **Awareness, Desire, Knowledge, Ability, and Reinforcement** (**ADKAR**) are being used to help provide insight and highlight potential problems with the ultimate adoption and success of any project. The contention is, if sufficient emphasis is not placed on understanding *what is in it* for the various stakeholders and/or the case for change is not understood and successfully communicated, the project itself becomes more difficult to manage, and the odds for success decrease significantly:

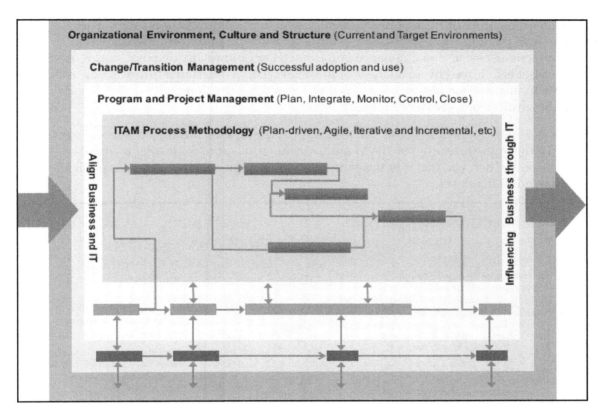

This schematic in the previous figure is my attempt to put all of this in context. I kept it at a conceptual level and I understand that in agile methods such as Scrum, connectivity does exist between the stakeholders and the team via the product owner and that user stories provide a vision of the end state, so don't take the connecting arrows too literally. What I hope you take away from this is the interconnectivity of the approaches and the synergy that can be gained by taking a more holistic approach. *Don't lose sight of the change management activities that can be the difference between a good ITAM/SAM program solution and a great one.*

ITAM/SAM is often under construction, with the principles of project management in frequent. Improvements designed to deliver savings, reduce risk, and improve financial performance require the involvement of multiple business units, systems, and the gathering of disparate data and processes. However, the use of project management principles is only a portion of the real application that happens daily through IT and software asset management.

Consider the nature of IT asset life cycle management. The project of managing an asset begins with planning and acquisition of the asset and continues through receiving, deployment, usage, and maintenance of the asset. Decommission, disposal, and retirement of the asset is followed by an analysis of the asset type, to determine future needs. All of these activities and events can be mapped out on a timeline, along with dependencies, sub-activities, milestones, and a critical path.

There is a huge opportunity to improve ITAM/SAM program and project success rates and to make the implementation of ITAM more meaningful and make lasting increases dramatically when you factor in the concepts of change management at the organization and the individual level.

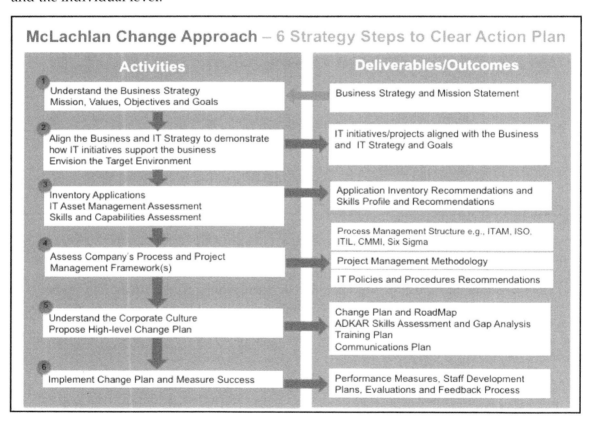

The McLachlan Change Approach is a six part strategy that converts the concepts of successful change management into a clear action plan

Don't make ITAM the red-headed stepchild during change management

As the famous Russian writer Leo Tolstoy said, *Everyone thinks of changing the world, but no one thinks of changing himself.* Similarly, multinational organizations talk about changing their business, but rarely do they change the internal processes from top to bottom.

The awful truth about change management is that most people and companies overuse the term without fully understanding what it is, the impact and how to approach organizations or individual groups in a structured approach. IT asset management plays a crucial role, but is often set aside prior to completion due to a variety of factors.

An overwhelming issue that crops up during most change management programs is the failure to institute a holistic IT asset management program from beginning to end. In many cases, the budget is cut or the focus of the IT or operational team is shifted elsewhere. What needs to be understood by IT asset managers and the executive suite (and even the board of directors) during this time of transformation are the enormous opportunities and long-term benefits each ITAM set provides. If you're heading up the ITAM initiative during an organizational change process, make sure that your program is not treated as the red-headed stepchild.

There are four major ITAM cross-functional activities that can significantly impact the organizational change activities:

1. **Program and project management**: While senior executives might have bought in on the fact that there needs to be a significant change management process, they likely do not realize the impact of this decision on all aspects of the company. In all likelihood, they have nearly zero understanding of the yeoman's effort IT will need to make to turn the ship 180 degrees. They might understand it from an overall strategic and operational viewpoint but, the fact is that other priorities in their purview, like shareholder management, company vision and direction, and so on—often trump this initiative. The first step is to ensure a strategic program and project management plan is created and presented in language the senior executives understanding including cost analysis, ROI, and ROI milestones. Next, a program management team needs to be carefully selected to oversee, manage, and act as the decision-making body for any strategic decisions. Within the program plan, project management teams should be formed with a clear understanding of defined roles and responsibilities (including the person accountable for each project).

Consider initiating a top to bottom IT asset management program so that initial cost savings or cost avoidance results can be shown immediately to senior executives. Outright financial savings or avoiding financial liabilities are understood and respected by the C-suite. Without their support, the ITAM program is destined to fail and IT will be paying somewhere between 30-45% more due to its assets and process inefficiencies. And, if the ITAM program is unsuccessfully implemented, there is no doubt that operational issues will crop up in the near and long-term from issues having to do with compliance, data management, IT service management, and day-to-day operations. Change will most certainly happen, but not for the better in this case.

2. **IT asset management becomes critical**: As with many enterprise changes, the likelihood is that employees will be shifted to different roles or, in a worst case scenario, downsized. The unfortunate reality of organizational change is the opportunity senior management takes to weed out employees that may not have progressed, did not keep up with current skills or are not ideal employees. So, during the entire change management process, there is a great deal of fluctuation with human resources resulting in major changeability for IT assets. This is the time for asset managers at all levels to create and/or revise as well as implement various aspects of an ITAM program and show ROI results:
    - Disposal management
    - Documentation management
    - Asset identification
    - Software asset management / Software license compliance

3. **Communications and education**: After spending months or even years on a corporate transformation, without proper communications and education, change often falls flat. Unfortunately, this is the most overlooked part of ITAM. Any good change management program—especially, with IT asset managers—should start off with building awareness and the desire for change as well as a good ongoing training program with each step of the change process. A few of the benefits are as follows:
    - Projects will more likely stay on time and budget.
    - Managers will more readily provide resources and sponsorship of the whole change process if they are involved upfront and understand what is happening. Team leads and middle management are the key to bringing about support. For example, if they realize the cost savings that a centralized SAM procurement process will have on their budget, they are less likely to criticize the adjustment even if it means obtaining their software apps at a slower pace.

- Overall employee-wide resistance will decrease. More often than not, the decrease is significant. Providing sound, rationale-supporting facts on why changes are happening and the step-by-step process involved, will likely bring about support and understanding.

4. **Policy and procedures**: After any modification—great or small—but especially, during an organizational change process, it is imperative to create and instill the correct policies and procedures to ensure ongoing compliance. Without either, the changes made within the organization will most certainly fail. And, once policies are in place—whether new or revised—the communications and education process begins all over again.

Think of the steps needed for change management as a caterpillar turning into a butterfly. With each stage of natural change, there are a group of controlled processes that must occur in order to move to the next phase and then, ultimately, to the final desired future state outcome (the final process of change management). The 12 process stages of ITAM should be in lock-step with each corporate and operational change to the organization. And, in fact, IT asset managers should seek these projects in order to become the corporate superhero—by showing significant cost savings to creating new operational efficiencies to decreasing and mitigating risk.

IBM Global Business Services conducted a worldwide survey among 500 multinational and public sector organizations and concluded that 9 of the 10 greatest barriers to change are people-related. The survey reinforces the perspective that it is not generally the lack of a formal project plan that causes projects to fail, although not following a plan is certainly an issue and having an unrealistic plan makes an appearance in the list. However, the majority of factors that cause a project to fail are tied to managing the expectations of individuals and dealing with company culture and politics.

Statements are made in meetings to the following effect:

- *We don't have the resources to implement any changes, people are fully occupied just dealing with day-to-day operational work*
- *These changes sound fine in theory but we will never be allowed to work this way, once we miss a target date the only thing that matters to management is getting back on schedule*
- *We don't have the skills to do this and we can never get training, every year we put training in the budget and every year it gets removed*
- *We have so much work to do we can never meet the timeline recommended for implementing the change, we will need to move much more slowly*

It is precisely because of these types of comments that change management becomes critical in supporting a project or change program. Remember, just because you can build it, doesn't mean anyone will use it!

Most change barriers are people-related:

Top Ten Barriers to Change	
Competition for limited resources	48%
Strong functional boundaries	44%
Limited change skills	43%
Resistance by middle management	38%
Long lead times for IT equipment	35%
Poor initiative communications	35%
Employee opposition	33%
HR (training/people) issues	33%
Organizational fatigue	32%
Unrealistic project plans / timetables	31%

Success factors are also linked to people:

Percentage of 500 Companies	
Ensuring top sponsorship	82%
Treating people fairly	82%
Involving employees	75%
Giving quality communications	70%
Providing sufficient training	68%
Using clear performance measures	65%
Building teams after change	62%
Focusing on culture/skill changes	62%
Rewarding success	60%
Using internal champions	60%

Conversely, comments you will hear after a successful project are more likely to be as follows:

- *It was clear what the focus of the project and team was-and if there was any doubt we had it posted on every bulletin board in the company.*
- *This was the CEO's baby and we all knew it was not going to be allowed to fail.*
- *Everyone was involved in the decision and felt their voices had been heard. Even if they did not agree with all of the aspects of the change, people knew it was the right thing to do.*
- *People were not just told this was going to happen they were trained to know how to make it successful.*

Change management complements good project management:

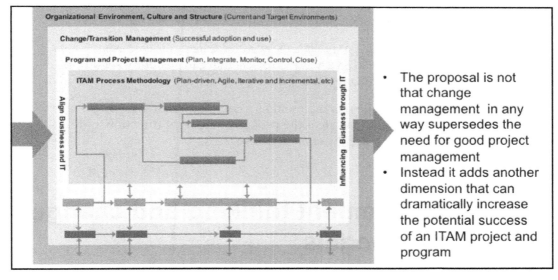

Change management

Highlights of this section

- Change management is the work stream dedicated to all of the people-related aspects of a project
- The focus is on gaining acceptance and support for the technical project work or outcomes
- Change management helps the people in the organization transition from the old environment to the new environment
- It complements good project management
- Change management focuses on putting mechanisms in place that will help to embed the change in the organization

The natural inclination of project managers is to focus on delivering an agreed-upon project outcome, on time, to budget, and within an agreed cost. However, that alone does not equate to a successful project.

The acid test is, "*does it provide the expected benefits for the business and is it being used?*" There are very few projects that purposefully set out to develop shelfware, but often that the end result.

Focusing on change management as a complement to the project management skills can steer the project in the right direction and significantly increase the chances for success.

Change management thinking and change management models

Okay, so if the problems on projects can be linked to ensuring that the people aspects of the work are given due attention, *what do we need to look at?*

In this section of the book, we will cover the concepts of change underlying management and provide some examples of why these are important.

We will also suggest two approaches/models to change management that can be used to identify areas of concern and potential outcomes and activities that can be used to complement an ITAM project plan.

The paradox principles

Thinking about ITAM project success from a change management perspective requires an understanding of the current environment and culture and that of the target environment and culture.

Addressing these issues forces you to deal with a number of potential paradoxes:

1. Positive change requires significant stability
2. To build an enterprise, focus on the individual
3. Focus directly on culture, indirectly
4. True empowerment requires forceful leadership
5. In order to build, you must tear down

(Source: *Price Waterhouse Change Integration Team-The Paradox Principles*)

Back in 1995, *The Change Integration* team within *Price Waterhouse Management Consulting Services* published *The Paradox Principles*. The book was subtitled *How high performance companies manage chaos, complexity and contradiction to achieve superior results*. The book was based on interviews with over 200 executives of Fortune 500 companies and is still highly relevant today.

I have paraphrased the following five principles:

1. Not everything changes, and to be successful in implementing change in an organization, focus equally on leveraging those areas that remain stable.

2. Changes impact organizations and people-of the two, the people side of the equation is the more critical to the success of the project; ignore it at your peril.

3. You need to understand how people think about a company and how they act within the company, what the company ethos is (the fundamental character or spirit of a culture; the underlying sentiment that informs the beliefs, customs, or practices of a group or society; dominant assumptions of a people or period) and how can you can build on this to improve your chances of success.

4. There is a lot of talk about empowering people and teams, for example, making them more customer-focused and having them take responsibility for goals and achievements. However, this does not come easily to many people and or teams and the responsibility falls to the leadership within the organization to prepare people to take on this new role. Projects that impact new and existing roles (and that is pretty much all of them) need to take this into consideration in planning the ITAM project implementation.

5. You have to be prepared to move away from existing ways of working and organizational structures if you want to change the way things are done, so in order to build, you must tear down.

Principle 1 – positive change requires significant stability

- If everything around you is constantly changing, then nothing gets done
- Some things need to be consistent, for example, communications
- Identify those areas within the organization where things should not change and emphasize them as ways of building trust in the change itself
- Areas to consider are as follows:
  - Culture (core values are unlikely to change)
  - Strategy (aligning the business and the vision)
  - People (visionary, catalyst, cooperator, stabilizer)
  - Core competencies (what it is you do as an organization)
  - Relationships (customers, suppliers, competitors)

People are wary of change, and so it is important to underline what is going to change and what will not be impacted by any ITAM changes.

Unless it is a major business transformation project where the entire mission or corporate goal(s) of the organization is changing (and that is a possible, but it would be a major change management project!) then it is worth reinforcing where the outcomes from the ITAM program will impact the business and emphasize how the project is supportive of the business vision and highlight the benefits it will provide.

Clearly, where people's roles and jobs are impacted, this is more sensitive, but no one is going to think that it will be business as usual if you are implementing a new project, so the more open you can be in discussing the change and can discuss options for those that are impacted, such as re-training or re-locating, the better.

What should be emphasized and should be consistent in any communications is that the business mission is not changing, the new ITAM program and project will strengthen the business, there is a need for this change and that work is underway to smooth any transition from the current environment to the target. What is actually being done to work with the people in departments that are impacted may not be something that is shared in a general communication, but needs to be addressed and will be part of an informal grapevine is if it is not handled by the project team.

Principle 2 – to build an ITAM enterprise, focus on the individual

- Organizations don't act; groups don't decide; individuals do
- Every outstanding team gathers talented individuals who work together to achieve an objective
- Just forming a team and declaring them as empowered is not enough-everyone on the team must be fully committed and accountable to attaining the objectives of the team:
  - Hire big people
  - Measure the team; reward the individuals
  - Search out and promote passionate leaders and effective coaches
  - Support the team and the individual with technology
  - Maximize the potential of the individual

What this is saying is that, for many organizations, the real value they provide comes from the people they employ. This is particularly true in industries such as consulting where best practices and tool knowledge is important, but the real assets are their people.

On the project team, *do you have the right people with the right skills and attitudes to get the work done?*

In the parts of the organization impacted by the ITAM project, have you identified those people who understand why the work is being done (those that really get it!) and *will champion and mentor others to make the project successful?*

If you don't have the right skills in place today, *do you have a plan in place to bring in or build the necessary skills sets? Have you considered what tools the team will need, and are they trained in using them?*

Finally, for all the people on the project team and those impacted by the results of the project, *have you considered what they need to be successful, and what would motivate them to make the project successful?*

Principle 3 – true empowerment requires forceful leadership

- Teams will work more efficiently when they are committed and empowered to make decisions:
    - Create the environment where team members can make decisions and be responsive to customer needs
    - Develop a high performing and passionate team
    - Be clear about who makes what decisions
- There needs to be a clear change leader on the project
- The change leader is responsible for ensuring the goals of the organizations are met, not that milestones are achieved
- The change leader is usually the project sponsor or their delegate, not the project manager

There are a few different dimensions to consider related to this principle.

From a project team perspective, *are roles clearly identified and does everyone know what their responsibilities are?* For example, for agile project development, *are the roles of the product owner, scrum master, and team member well defined?*

For the people *who will take over the operation of the delivered project, have new roles, responsibilities, and job descriptions been defined? Is training being developed to help those people understand what is expected of them going forward, and how does this tie in to any reward systems?*

Who has the ultimate responsibility for ensuring that the outcomes of the project meet the needs of the business? This doesn't mean that the project has met its milestones, but that the business benefits are realized! This is the role of the change leader-the person in the business who is committed to the success of the project and will remove the barriers to success. It may be a key stakeholder and it may be necessary to have someone work with them throughout the project as an advisor, but it is a key role in the success of any project.

Principle 4 – focus directly on culture, indirectly

- Culture is the way we do things around here; it describes the values, behaviors, and attitudes that typify an organization
- A number of factors influence and an organization's culture:
    - Leadership actions
    - Performance measures

- People practices (*are the right people promoted?*)
- Vision, purpose, and strategy
- Organizational structure
- You need to communicate the culture you want to have

There is a lot that has been written on culture and culture change, yet it remains an under-appreciated area. In the strategic execution framework developed by Stanford University and featured in their course on *Converting Strategy into Action*, one of the key pillars to success is understanding and leveraging a company's culture.

Do people turn up for meetings? Do they pay attention or are they on their laptops the whole time? Do managers have offices? How are people measured in the organization? What is important in getting ahead? Is it a functionally-driven organizational structure or is it project/team-driven or a matrix organization?

Understanding how your company works (and understanding if the intent is to change this) will impact what the project team produces. For example, a very hierarchical structured organization may require detailed work procedures and processes, whereas a more fluid project-based structure may require higher level instructions but may need a mentoring program to ensure the project is considered complete, and it will impact the estimates and planned activities.

Principle 5 – in order to build, you must tear down

- The structures and processes that got you where you are today are not necessarily the ones that will get you to where you want to be in the future
- The real measures of success for an organization may be very different from what is being measured today
- To develop really effective measures, get rid of a lot of them
- Measure processes and results as part of a balanced scorecard
- After the change has occurred, jobs may well have also changed, and these roles need to be defined
- Project work is becoming more critical as organizations respond to the need for change-measuring a person's ability to work as part of a project can yield interesting results

What will the business look like when the project has successfully delivered? How can you measure success? If you don't measure today or if the measures are going to change, you need a start with a baseline.

What is in place today as performance measures may not be how you want to judge the business in the future, so the concept is to be prepared to jettison current performance measures, organizational structures, and ways of working to get to where you want to be in the future.

There is a saying, *what got you into the position you are in today is unlikely to be able to get you out in the future.* And that is used as a rationale for wholesale change. I think this is overly simplistic; there are a number of inter-connected reasons why an organization reaches the point when they want to make a change and you need to assess what has worked and what has not. But, going back to the first principle, make sure you keep what works and focus on what needs to change.

Finally, from a personnel perspective, as more project-based work becomes the norm (or at least is the target), consider the individuals in the organization and how well they work as part of a team. It is a different dynamic than just being able to do their work.

Organizing the change management activities into logical phases of work:

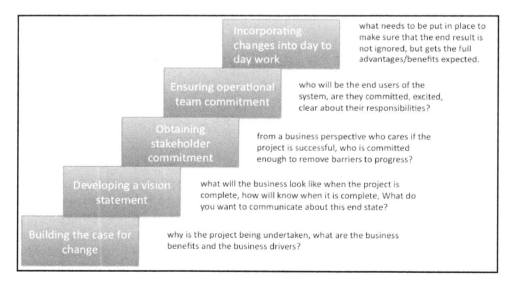

So, the paradox principles make you think about the people aspects of the project, but *how do you organize that thinking into logical phases of work?* One way to do this is to think about the milestones that need to be achieved.

While the paradox principles are not a linear set of processes, the milestones and outcomes they produce can be organized into a logical life cycle or building block type framework are as follows:

1. Building the case for change, based on paradox principle 1—*what needs to change and what doesn't?*
2. Developing a vision statement, based on paradox principle 5—*what structures and outcomes do you want to see in the new environment and what do you want to get rid of?*
3. Obtaining stakeholder commitment, based on paradox principle 3—*have you identified a change leader within the organization?*
4. Ensuring operational team commitment, based on paradox principle 2—*do you have a high performing team; if not, what can you do about it?*
5. Incorporating changes into day-to-day work, based on paradox principle 4—*how do you ensure the changes will be accepted within the culture of the organization?*

There is precedent for this type of model—GE change acceleration process:

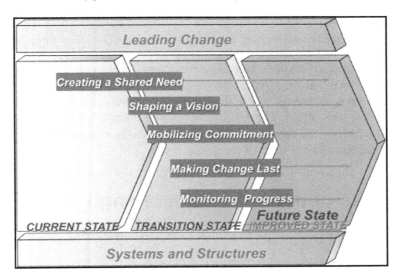

The proprietary model used by GE demonstrates very similar sets of activities but with more emphasis on leading change and the underlying systems and structures.

Here's one more perspective on change:

The **ADKAR** framework (Jeffrey M Hiatt) focuses on the individual, but can be used to complement project-level changes are as follows:

- A - Awareness
- D - Desire
- K - Knowledge
- A - Ability
- R - Reinforcement

Which paradox principle does this remind you of?

Another way to think about change management is to take a model that focuses on the individual. One such model is ADKAR.

It is a very clear and useful model that makes you think about why you are doing things. So, you may decide based on the thought processes coming out of the paradox principles that, to get people committed and to support a project's outcomes, you need a communications strategy. What ADKAR makes you think about is:

- Who are you trying to communicate with?
- What do you want them to know?
- Are you simply trying to build awareness, or do you want them to take action?

If it is the latter, is a communications message sufficient, or do you have to get more personal and think about training programs? Basically, you are looking at what's in it for the individual, and then, how you move them from awareness of the project to the point where they want to get involved. Then, think about what knowledge they need to be able to do the work and how you can establish an environment where that knowledge can be put into practice and become a new way of working.

A – awareness of the need for a change

- What is the nature of the change and how does the change align with the vision for the organization?
- What are the risks of not changing?
- How will the change impact our organization or our community?
- What's in it for me (WIIFM)?

- While building awareness is not only about communications, having a communications strategy is essential and should include the following:
  - The audience groups
  - Messages to be sent
  - Timing, channels, and packaging
  - Who will send communications

The first step in the ADKAR model is building awareness of the change. That seems simple, but recognizing that you are focused on awareness and fighting the temptation to put too much into the messages helps you create a more meaningful and directed message.

In the awareness stage of the process you also need to think about what it is that people need to be aware of.

How easy will it be to build the right level of awareness? You need to consider factors such as the following:

- How well things are working today? (if you are focused at an individual level, how well the individual feels things are working today. This can change the message.)
- How an organization/individual deals with problems/change?
- The credibility of the person delivering the message-should the message come from the CEO, the department leader, or someone closer to the project
- What they may have already heard, rumors, and so on
- Ease of understanding why the change is needed

D – desire—willingness to engage in and support a change

- More difficult to address as it involves changing how other people think about an issue

- Builds on awareness, but acceptance and positive support depends on the following:
    - How the individual views the change (opportunity or threat)?
    - How seriously the organization takes the change and their track record of making changes?
    - Individuals' personal circumstances
    - Personal motivators or inhibitors
    - How the message is communicated

OK, so once you are past the Awareness stage, then the appropriate audiences know a change is coming and should understand why the change is being made and what the risks are of not changing. The next step is to answer the question, so what do you want me to do about it?

The messages here are starting to get more focused on individuals and teams and are all about people's willingness to support the change. In this stage, there is a need to think about which stakeholders are committed and which are merely involved in the process. Do you have the right stakeholders on board?

At the level where people's roles will be impacted by the change there is a need to think about what's in it for them and to develop messages specifically aimed at these individuals - potentially on a one-on-one basis.

This is also where corporate culture becomes more visible—how successful has the company been with past changes? Or is this another one where those impacted feel if they keep their heads down, this will fade away like earlier initiatives?

K – knowledge—how to implement the change

Knowledge focuses on developing materials that are needed to explain to an individual how to operate in the changed environment.

- Training and education needed to develop new skills and ways of working
- Documentation of new processes, procedures, systems, and the use of related tools
- Development of new job roles and descriptions in the changed environment

When you start to think about the Knowledge phase in ADKAR, you are starting to answer the question, how do I operate in the new changed world?

Assuming that the desire has been established, then people need to have the appropriate training, information, templates, and so on to work in the new environment. You need to take the following into consideration:

- Individual's current knowledge base
- Ability of an individual to learn
- Education available
- Access to required knowledge

This is an interesting area, as most project plans will take into account the training that is needed, but if this stage is undertaken and the desire stage has not been addressed, there is a real danger of the materials becoming shelf-ware.

A – ability—turning knowledge into action

- Knowing how to do something is not the same thing as being able to do it!
- Ability is demonstrating the capability to both implement the change and to do so at a desired performance level:
    - Psychological blocks
    - Physical abilities
    - Intellectual capability and/or inclination
    - Time to learn
    - Availability of resources (mentors, coaches, SMEs)
- Companies that turn knowledge into action avoid the smart talk trap; they inspire deeds, not just words. This is paraphrased from *The Knowing-Doing Gap* by *Jeffrey Pfeffer* and *Robert Sutton*

R – reinforcement factors needed to sustain a change

- Meaningful change is not a one-time event; changes need to be sustained and ideally evolve over time
- Recognition and rewards need to be meaningful to an individual
- Individuals and the organizations need to get a feeling of accomplishment when milestones are reached (celebrating small accomplishments)
- Reinforcement should lead to continuous improvement
- To balance the positives, there has to be a negative response for not changing

This is the phase where ADKAR discusses sustaining the change. It is where many projects lose sight of the ultimate benefits by implementing and not following through, yet this is where there is the greatest opportunity for seeing sustained benefits.

This phase ties into the evaluation process of a company and confirms that people are rewarded for making the change a success. If old measures are left in place it will, at the least, cause confusion, but more will more likely undermine the success of the project.

The use of dashboards to continue to monitor progress and the idea of lessons learned feedback sessions are all valuable tools to keep the changes current and alive.

Combining the two models into an ITAM change management matrix

Bringing this all together. One way to think about this is to build a matrix for the main lifecycle activities and then assess from an ADKAR perspective. The result is shown in the following table:

	Assessing the case for Change	Developing a Vision Statement	Obtaining Stakeholder Commitment	Ensuring Operational Team Commitment	Incorporating Changes into Day-to-day ways of work
Awareness	Craft the messages describing why a change is needed	Design and describe what will the change look like?	Develop a stakeholder Matrix	Expand the stakeholder Matrix to understand who else is impacted by the change	
	Undestand who is impacted by the change and develop a communications strategy	Demonstrate and communicate how the change supports business goals?	Identify the top project/business sponsor?	Develop a Targeted Communications Plan	
Desire		Define the business benefits associated with the change and what are the risks of not changing?	Dterine who will take ownership of the project to ensure the change is successful?	Involve the team in defining What's In It for Me (WIIFM) Operationally and Individually	
		Consider what will motivate people to want to adopt the change?	Plan how can you influence people that are not committed to the project success?	Document the target environment to illustrate how will things improve after the change?	
Knowledge			Develop performance measures and targets. Understanding the costs of getting people trained to use the new systems	Determine and Design the artifacts needed to enable the change e.g., training, processes, procedures, tools?	
Ability			Assist stakeholders in building an extended support structure for the change ?	Develop training curriculums and schedules, coaching and mentoring networks	Establish reinforcement training and learning events.
Reinforcement					Establish rewards, recognition programs, certifications, audits, etc to keep the focus on leveraging the change

Awareness is not a one-time set of actions; it is spread across the project and impacts multiple activities and groups.

Overall, the ADKAR activities build upon each other; in fact, there is an ADKAR profile that can be developed that will help show where some of the ADKAR actions have been missed and where there are potential weak points in a project.

In the second part of this, you will see some techniques that can be used to drive out actions for each stage in the ITAM change management process.

Highlights of this sections are as follows:

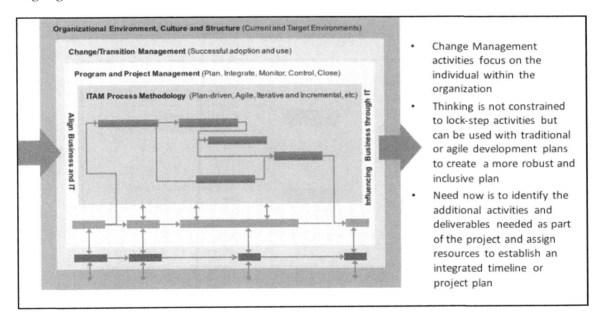

ITAM change management process

Assessing the case for change

Is the rationale for the change obvious?

- Expand on the question, why are we doing this?
- Is there a burning platform?

- Does everyone understand the reason for the change?
- Could they articulate why a change is needed?
- Are the outcomes of the change initiative understood in terms of changes in ways of working and/or impact on the company culture?
- Is there an understanding of how the change supports the overall business strategy?

The rationale for making a change is generally understood, but not necessarily by all of the people impacted. If you asked everyone impacted why a change is being made or a new project is underway, the likelihood is you will end up with as many answers as people.

Also, the scale of a change is usually not well understood, and just *how much of a change will it be?* In this section, we look at some techniques for visually depicting the degree of change.

For a project to be seen as relevant, it needs to be aligned to the overall business objectives:

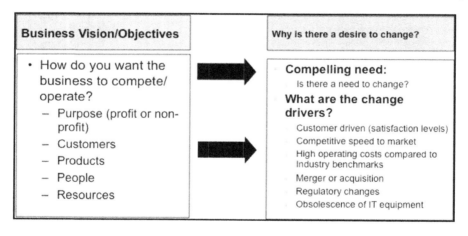

In project terms, *what is the motivation for the project?*

Identify the change drivers from interviews with C-levels in the organization—*where do they want to take the organization and what is holding them back?*

Take a portfolio management view of the organization:

- Align the mission and business objectives of the organization to the current initiatives.
- Does this mapping highlight gaps that will be addressed by the proposed project(s)?

- Is there a clear linkage between the proposed projects and the business objectives? If not, then question why is the project being undertaken?

Organization Mission/Value Statements	Business Objectives	Strategy/Goals	Projects
Focus on optimizing stakeholder value for clients	Build and strengthen Business Partnering Relationships (trusted advisor)		
Provide Industry expertise to help solve clients toughest enterprise business problems		Demonstrable and consistent ways of working, aligned to Industry standards	possible ITIL Implementatation in IT Department ?

What needs to change?

- How do you see the organization operating differently in the future?
- What are the main dimensions of change?
- How can you represent this visually, so that the degree of change is evident?

Take an example of a company that has an IT department that has grown organically over the years with the company and is focused mostly on *keeping the lightson* and fire-fighting using mostly in-house personnel that have been with the company since its inception.

The business side of the company is frustrated with the fact that they want IT to become a partner in helping them implement new technology to evolve the business and keep them competitive, so basically, they want to move the thinking in IT away from an operational (business as usual, support) mode to a strategic, project-based mindset. At the same time, they are questioning if the current IT personnel have the ability to make the transition in a timely manner or at all, so there is a dimension of change that addresses the sourcing of IT services from in-house to potentially outsourcing, SaaS, co-sourcing, and so on.

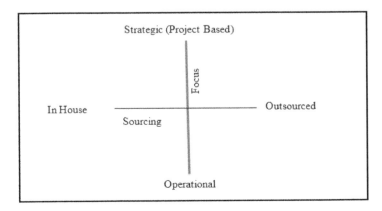

One way of helping to frame the scope of the change is to plot the dimensions of change and show where on a continuum the existing organization is and then where it wants to be.

Understanding the quadrants?

- You need to develop a map for where you are today and where you want to be.
- In the following image, name each quadrant—so, for example, the bottom left quadrant indicates an organization *where the drivers are clear tasks and work is conducted by internal teams (basically, order takers), but what about the others?*

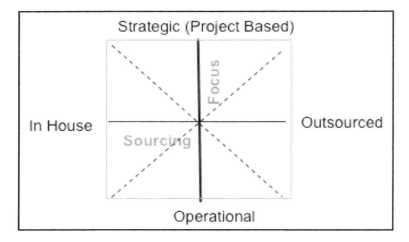

Mark a position on the dotted lines where the organization is today by using a sliding scale starting at zero where the lines cross in the middle of the diagram, and moving out to 5 or 10 depending on how granular you feel at the outer reaches of the line.

Join up the marks for the current state, and you end up with something resembling an egg. Then, if you overlay the target state, you can see the difference between where you want to be and where you are today. Refer the following image.

Where is the business today, and where does it want to be?

The blue oval represents where the organization is today, and the red oval indicates where they want to be:

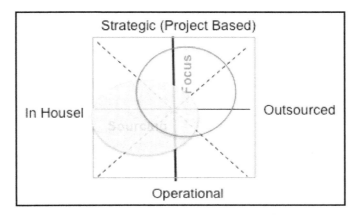

Exercise:

- Develop a current and target model for an existing project. Either select one of your own, or use this one.
- A successful IT hardware and system software company wants to change direction to focus on providing turnkey solutions for their customers/clients, leveraging the most appropriate tools and hardware to resolve the client's issues. Two dimensions of change they need to model are as follows:
    - Organizational structure ranging from a functional product model to a matrix project-based model.
    - Skillset changes moving from a technical SME to an independent business partner.
- Draw the current and target profiles of the organization.

In this section of the chapter, we will discuss developing an ITAM vision statement.

What is the purpose of an ITAM vision statement?

Take a look at the following image:

What is the value of a vision statement?

- To explain why it is important to the business to make a change
- To answer the question "where do we want to be?"
- To highlight areas that will need to change
- To ensure there is a shared understanding of the need for the change
- To identify potential champions
- To understand early if there is likely to be any major resistance

What are you looking for in a vision?

- Expressed with optimism and emotion
- Seen as being worthwhile and "worth the risk"
- Customer focused
- Challenging, motivating & energizing
- Easy to understand
- Actionable
- Everyone gets it!
- End result focused

The vision statement expands upon the decision that a change is needed and paints a high-level picture of where we want to be when the change is complete. It is the simple (possibly) mantra that everyone understands in a shared fashion and can explain. Even if they have some concerns about how the change is going to be implemented, they should be in agreement that a change is needed.

The value of a vision statement can be understood when you consider the confusion that Leo Apotheker created in the market and internally in HP when he announced they were getting out of the PC market. The question then became, so *what is the market that HP are aiming at?* In contrast, when IBM took over PwC Consulting in 2002, Sam Palmisano was clear that this was IBM going full-bore to the solutions marketplace. IBM was expanding beyond hardware and infrastructure. It is also interesting that the vision was so clear that hardly anyone mentioned it when IBM sold their PC business to Lenovo.

Making a vision actionable:

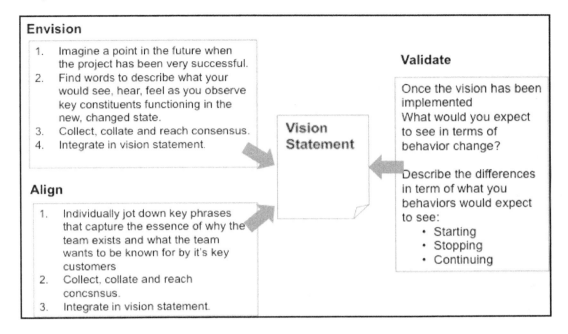

Crafting a shared vision

Consider where you want to be at the end of the ITAM change program and *what that will look like internally and externally,* and both short and long term:

A SWOT analysis can offer helpful perspectives at any stage of an effort. You might use it to explore potential new efforts or solutions to problems. It can help you to make decisions about the best path for your ITAM initiative. Identifying your opportunities for success in the context of threats to success can clarify directions and choices. Determine where change is possible. If you are at a junction or turning point, an inventory of your strengths and weaknesses can reveal priorities as well as opportunities. Adjust and refine plans mid-course. A new opportunity might open wider avenues, while a new threat could close a path that once existed. SWOT also offers a simple way of communicating about your ITAM initiative or program and an excellent way to organize information you've gathered from studies or surveys.

SWOT analysis can also be used as a TOWS model focusing more on external perspectives. In this model, it can be looked at as a threats and opportunity matrix, where you consider potential changes as both a threat and an opportunity, both short and long-term.

Having determined what you want to achieve, consider the best way to implement the vision:

Here's an explanation of the three Ds matrix:

- **Demand** refers to the degree to which senior management or others can simply demand that change occurs (such as releasing held inventory or announcing a radical realignment of the organization).
- **Data/Diagnosis** refers to the degree to which internal and/or external sources of data frame the need change (such as benchmarking or competitive data).
- **Demonstration** refers to the role that best practice sites or pilot projects can play in creating the need for change.

Exercise: Validating the vision

- *How confident do you feel that each team member would deliver essentially the same message regarding the need for change if asked by someone outside of the team?*
- Imagine stepping into an elevator with a key stakeholder, for a 60-second ride.
- How would you respond to the questions:
  - *Why are you doing this project?*
  - *What is the business benefit?*
  - *How do you know when you are done?*
  - *How do you know if you have a good outcome, not just any outcome?*

The last two questions are simple, yet two of the most powerful questions to ask about any project.

Bill Smilie references these in his book *Great Question! Reflections on Professional, Project, and Organizational Performance.*

Keeping these questions in the forefront of your thinking is a great way to avoid the trap of becoming caught up in the project work without keeping the end goal in mind. If you've gone to the trouble of developing a vision, then it needs to drive the work and not just be an elegant discussion document!

Now, we will discuss obtaining stakeholder commitment:

Executive stakeholders

Having the right executive sponsor is the most often cited reason for a successful project. Executive stakeholders are the people within the organization that have the responsibility and desire to make the project successful. They are the visible figureheads of the project that are prepared to stand behind the project and actively show their sponsorship in the following ways:

- Communicating the vision of the ITAM program/project to all of the interested parties
- Demonstrating an active interest in success by heading the steering committee for the ITAM project
- Building and managing an extended group of supporters across the organization

These are the people who are committed to the success of the project and not just involved because of their role or position in the organization. A strong executive stakeholder can assist with creating and strengthening relationships within the organization in order to assist the ITAM project, and manage expectations with other stakeholders.

Stakeholder management

Stakeholder analysis is the task of assessing key stakeholders and their issues with respect to the change. Stakeholder analysis provides important input for your ITAM change management approach:

- To know your stakeholder groups (their profile, their concerns, their expectations, the channels to reach them)
- To identify the range of interests that need to be taken into consideration in planning change
- To update the vision and change process to generate the best support for the project
- To set up your communication strategy and plan

How do you assess which stakeholders are the ones that are most committed? Hopefully, it is obvious, but sometimes you need to test if the people most appropriately positioned are really the ones that wield the most influence on the success of the project.

How can you do the following:

- Establish a two-way communication process
- Develop a process to detect fearful or negative reactions that could hinder the change effort
- Manage resistance to change
- Maximize positive engagement

Stakeholder analysis

The following screenshot shows the stakeholder analysis:

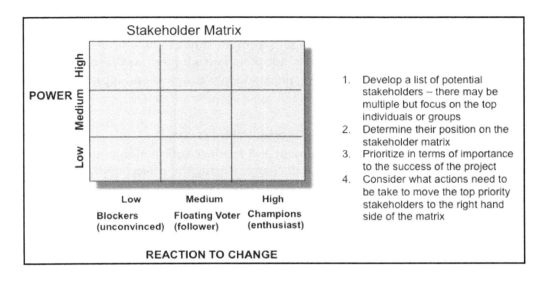

Stakeholder Matrix

1. Develop a list of potential stakeholders – there may be multiple but focus on the top individuals or groups
2. Determine their position on the stakeholder matrix
3. Prioritize in terms of importance to the success of the project
4. Consider what actions need to be take to move the top priority stakeholders to the right hand side of the matrix

Mobilizing commitment – attitude charting

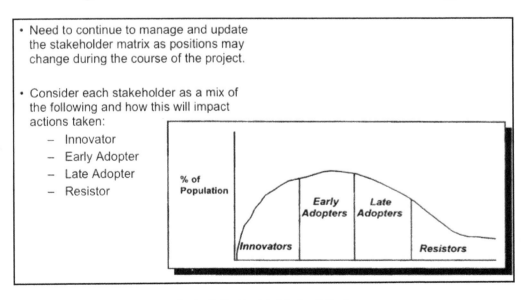

- Need to continue to manage and update the stakeholder matrix as positions may change during the course of the project.

- Consider each stakeholder as a mix of the following and how this will impact actions taken:
    - Innovator
    - Early Adopter
    - Late Adopter
    - Resistor

Based on Geoffrey Moore's book Dealing with Darwin

How you interact with the stakeholder or stakeholder groups will be partially determined by where they fit on a maturity model ranging from the innovators—those that are excited to take on new ideas and changes—to early adopters/late adopters and resistors. See *Moore's* book for the lag between early adopters and late adopters and typical percentages.

Highlights of this section:

- A strong executive stakeholder is essential for success
- Assessing stakeholder commitment and levels of satisfaction is an on-going activity stakeholder attitudes will change during the project and/or their interests may vary

In this section of the chapter, we will go over how to ensure operational team commitment.

Establishing a winning team

Others beyond the executive stakeholder in the organization have to demonstrate commitment for an ITAM program and project to be successful:

- **Project team**: You cannot just co-opt people onto the team; if they are not committed, it will be apparent and will undermine success
- **Peer managers**: they need to accept the importance of the project and support the priority assigned to the work against competing projects
- **End users**: People who work with the outcomes/new processes on a daily basis need to understand the value of the work and ultimately need to know how to use the outcomes more effectively
- **Customers**: They need to see that the end results are aligned with the success of the business and improve the quality of the service or product being provided
- **Risk Managers**: They need to be advocates of the project and should promote the changes as being ways to better manage risk (or at least not increase risks)
- **HR**: *Should view the project as beneficial for the business and employees*
- *Others?*

Thoughts on stakeholder assessments

Middle managers are a vital but often ignored group; they are seen as a problem rather than a point of leverage. The best *case for change* will lead employees to see that the proposed road ahead is better than the alternatives (including standing still). Two hours of genuine involvement are worth 10 hours of one-way communication. The grapevine will fill any communication vacuum; the distortion of the message will be high, and people will believe what they want to believe. The most underrated principle in change programs is the fair treatment of employees and how to make it happen.

 Resistance to change is natural and not always a bad thing

Separate positive from negative resistance

Positive Resistance (Testing the Change)	Negative Resistance (Push back)
Open-minded questioning Disagreeing with the solution Lobbying for alternative solutions Analyzing and appraising alternatives Questioning the need Challenging the vision	Not attending meetings Being too busy to attend training Pulling key people out of workshops Starting another initiative Questioning the budget Having a phantom initiative Ignoring the initiative
What can you do?: Listen and be prepared to discuss particularly the solution Support if appropriate at the visioning stages Challenge if the issues are related to why the project is being undertaken	**What can you do?:** Understand that there will be some resistance and look for ways to mitigate concerns, but do not spend too much time resolving the problems of few if this is distracting from the overall success Be prepared to use the Executive Sponsor

Recognize the difference between involvement and commitment:

	Involved in the Change	Committed to the Change
Awareness	Understand why the change is being made and what it involves	Understand why the change is being made and what it involves
Desire	Will comply with the change if I have to	Can see personal and/or organizational value of the change and wants to be part of it's success
Knowledge	Tell me in detail what I need to do	What can I do to get access to the materials that will help me make the change successful?
Ability	Who do I ask when things go wrong?	What can I do to make sure things don't go wrong?
Reinforcement	What am I being measured against?	How do we build on the change to continually improve?

Difference between involvement and commitment

Exercise: Managing resistance – *what approaches could you try?*

High	Can't/Will	Can/Will
Willingness	Can't/Won't	Can/Won't
Low	Ability	High

Results: Managing resistance:

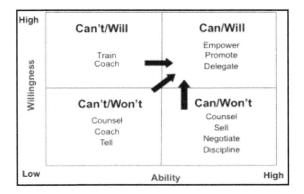

Results of managing resistance

Levels of commitment will influence the communication plan and channels

The level of commitment will help surface the communications challenges and in turn will suggest potential communications channels. The following diagram illustrates the types of involvement and commitment:

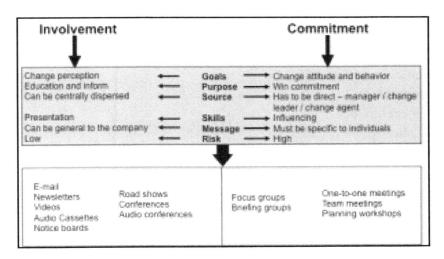

Types of involvement and commitment

Making ITAM change last

If you build it, they may not come! You can build an elegant solution to a business problem or opportunity, but if it is not used and does not continually adapt it, will fail over time. Every change initiative will compete for time, resources, and attention, and not just during the development cycle, but once it's implemented, it needs to be supported. In many cases, most of the effort is spent on launching initiatives rather than embedding the change into the fabric of the business. Changes to organizational systems and structures help make the change a natural part of the accepted ways of working.

How do you measure success?

There needs to be a baseline for comparison established early in the change process. Establish performance measures and targets early in the project. Monitor progress against key events and milestones to reward successes—make sure these milestones are clearly defined and are celebrated. Than, gather feedback from employees and other groups impacted by the change and adapt as needed. You want to build accountability mechanisms into the ITAM systems and structures, for example, ITAM performance evaluation reports:

- Ensure people know what to do and what is expected of them
- Conduct audits and communicate results

Performance measures and balanced scorecards

Measure processes as well as results. Establish targets and ranges. Map trends and ensure that all targets are SMART:

- Specific
- Measurable
- Achievable
- Realistic
- Timely

Summary

This chapter introduced a way of thinking about projects that is still result-oriented, but is equally focused on the people aspects of the projects and describes how taking a change management approach to your ITAM project's success brings the project to life for many people and moves them from understanding what is happening to being an active participant in the success of your organization's ITAM program.

I also covered whether it is a discrete activity, such as licensing a specific software package, or the ongoing effort of monitoring and insuring the health of the IT infrastructure. The information provided by an ITAM program is critical to the project goal of utilizing IT assets to their maximum potential within your organization. Organizations can save time, money, and improve the quality of the IT services by understanding the change and project management nature of IT asset lifecycle management processes and solutions.

In the next chapter, we will cover how to start your ITAM/SAM program, the policies, and processes you should have in place to help you be proactive in the management and control of your program.

8
Now What?

ITAM and SAM begins with a solid foundation of communication, policies, processes, and people, then the selection of a tool that provides the functionality required to meet the goals of your organization. Getting the most out of your program requires a strategic, holistic approach to implementation that supports and optimizes your ongoing efforts.

That is a mouthful. You've been tasked with doing all of that. You've learned from all the previous chapters what ITAM, SAM, software audits, contracts, and tools are all about. Now that you have all this information, now what? Let's say you've implemented and deployed your program and a tool. Your organization now has its ITAM/SAM program, tool, and key processes in place. You have the foundational policies needed in place that tell individuals employed by your organization, what is expected of them, what they must do, and what they can't do. You have everything you need now to manage this correctly. You do, but honestly, like most of my clients when I am ready to transition everything over to them, I always have the folks who have been tasked with the responsibility of managing ITAM/SAM asking me, *now what?* They are still stuck on *where do I start*?

To be exact, they ask me what their day to day should look like. Where do I begin? What exactly is expected of me? We all like to talk about high-level standards, processes, and many more things. Here, I am going to walk you through what your day(s) could look like in your Asset Manager role. Now, this doesn't mean you have to do it this way; use it as a guideline to find what feels right for you and your organization.

It's ok to feel overwhelmed, especially when you might have limited resources (budget, people, and so on). What I share with organizations and the individual(s) tasked to manage everything is to break tasks into buckets. Some tasks might require your attention daily, monthly, or quarterly. I also like to put what I share with them in the form of processes, so others know what to do if its more than one person in a team or if they have backups.

Be pragmatic. Go for what will make the biggest impact to your organization based on priorities. For example, do you need to address software license compliance or to mitigate other risks? Or do you need to just deal with normal ITAM activities. The following image shows that I have four tasks I want to manage: inventory, financial management, compliance and risk, and process performance.

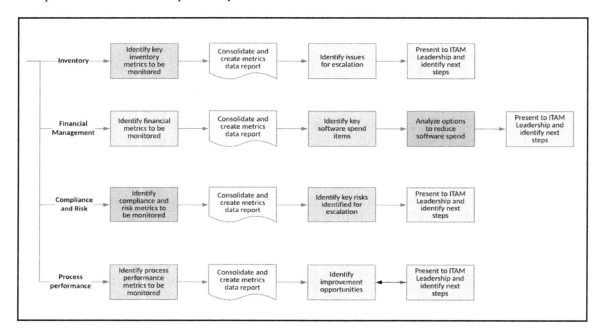

Another way to bucket tasks is to see what beneficial and key information would be of value to other teams within your organization.

Key information that would be of interest includes the following:

- Discovery of new IT assets (hard and soft) in the environment
- Software license and entitlement management
- Change in software usage
- Maintenance and renewals
- Unplanned incidents and events
- Software black-and-white list

Honestly, a big part of your role as Asset Manager is to link everyone together and promote transparency. Cross-departmental team interaction across your organization covering governance, organizational functions, including roles and responsibilities, will enable collaboration and support for your ITAM/SAM program.

Organizational functions	ITAM/SAM support
Procurement	• Requests • Orders • Receiving and asset-tagging
Contract and lease management	• Contracting negotiations • Contracting renewal • Amendments • Lease creation and maintenance
Finance	• Expense/cost allocation • Budget tracking • Depreciation • Total cost of ownership
Asset management	• Inventory • Asset deployment • Support and warranty • Software asset, license, and entitlement management • ITAM/SAM policy development • Communicate ITAM/SAM program and policies • IMAC • Disposal
Governance	• Defining technology standards • Defining configurations • Overseeing ITAM/SAM initiative • Enforcing ITAM/SAM policies
System management	• Investigating tools for infrastructure design • Evaluating solutions for infrastructure design • Implementing solution • Supporting solution • Integrating solution with other systems

Using ITAM, ITIL, and ISO industry standards to map out processes, functions, roles, and responsibilities begin with baselines, such as those shown in the following charts, and then developing customized structures based on each of your organizational goals and needs while following industry best practices. To ensure compliance with the selected standard, I recommend the establishment of a cross-functional quality and standards review board. Establish a **Corporate Advisory Board (CAB)**—stakeholders, use **Request for Change (RFC**s) to run proposed changes through the CAB and route the RFCs through stakeholders for impact analysis prior to being presented to the CAB.

For a software license management effort, the following stakeholders are sometimes involved:

- **Contract and vendor management**: Responsible for negotiating software license terms necessary to enable license transfer and proof of license.
- **ITAM program manager**: Overall responsibility for the program.
- **Infrastructure tools**: ITAM as well as any other leveraged tools, such as SCCM, ILMT, and so on.
- **Server group**: Agree to allow auto-discovery agents on servers, report server metrics that cannot be auto-discovered to support license calculations (for per-CPU type licenses).
- **Application owners**: As needed, to report other license metrics (such as # user accounts for per-named-user type licenses). Also, to support feeds from other source systems.
- **Infrastructure (workstation IMAC and data center IMAC)**: Responsible to make sure images include any agents required, and to follow prescribed processes.
- **Disposal vendor(s)**: To feed back-list of disposed assets to trigger final software license harvest (if not already done).
- **Executive leadership**: Reinforce new policies, overall program guidance, and governance.
- **Corporate communications**: To assist in communications of the program, newsletters, broadcast messaging, end user screen design, internal ITAM intranet site design, and so on.
- **Finance**: Assists with budgeting, costing, ROI, and so on.

Organizational roles and responsibilities based on the following ITAM Roles and Responsibilities can be customized to suit your specific needs based on what is currently in place at your organization, what would need to be implemented, and what would need to be revised/updated.

Depending on the size of your organization, you may or may not need all these roles.

ITAM Role Description	Responsibility & Knowledge/Skill Set	Process Tasks
Asset Manager	• Collaborate with management to define cost savings, asset compliances and service improvements. • Coordinate with management in utilizing the asset management tools to analyze, review and track asset data. • Manage asset reconciliation and asset disposal agreements. • Educate end-users on ITAM/SAM policies. • Prepare and manage IT asset capital and expense budgets. • Ensure audit compliance for IT assets.	• Design and execute asset management policies, procedures and processes. • Develop asset control processes to monitor accountability, identification, maintenance, location and contracts. • Assist in inventory management, procurement and reharvesting activities. • Assist in contract negotiation, contract renewals and vendor management activities. • Monitor software licenses to ensure they comply with license agreements and usage standards.
End User	• Has knowledge of request process, technology standards, approval cycles	• Uses e-forms, web-based interface, e-mail, or phone to request IT assets or services.
Request Management	• Has knowledge of technology standards, approval cycles	• Receives request, verifies against internal technology standards, financial requirements and approvals • Flags request as standard or exception • Routes exceptions to proper resources

Service Management	• Responsible for execution of processes for:
	   o Requests
	   o IMAC
	• Knowledge of Asset Lifecycle
		• Verifies asset availability
		• Initiates service order (IMAC)
		• Insures requests are moving and being worked on

ITAM Role Description	Responsibility & Knowledge/Skill Set	Process Tasks
Procurement / Vendor Management	• Responsible for execution of acquisition process • Knowledge of technology standards, approval flow • Develops purchasing policies and procedures • Vendor relationships • Product-line knowledge • Negotiation skills	• Receives request • Verifies approvals • Creates and maintains P.O. • Researches pricing & gets quote • Maintains vendor contacts and vendor contracts
Receiving	• Responsible for execution of the receiving process • Knowledge of receiving/return policies and procedures	• Takes care of deliveries • Prepares return of equipment
IMAC	• Responsible for execution of the IMAC process • Knowledge of IMAC policies and procedures, including decommission and disposal • Knowledge of technology standards	• Receives and prepares assets for deployment • Installs/Moves/Adds/Changes • Maintains IT asset data • Tags assets during configuration
Decommission	• Responsible for execution of the disposal process • Knowledge of lease agreements • Knowledge of fixed asset policies and procedures • Knowledge of software harvest and reuse policies and procedures	• Returns IT assets to lessors • Updates ITAM/SAM system with asset status information • Disposes of physical asset • Harvests software/software license
Financial Analysis	• Responsible for execution of the financial analysis process • Fixed assets, financial policies and procedures • Depreciation rules and recommends changes • Budgets & cost centers	• Maintains budget groups and cost centers • Compiles cost data for leadership
Software Management	• Responsible for execution of the software asset management process, software harvest and recycle process, entitlement management • Software product lines • Knowledge of technology standards • Software Audit Response	• Communicates software standards • Monitors license usage and compliance • Approves license allocation • Manages software license agreements
Contracts, Warranty, Maintenance Management	• Responsible for execution of the contract management process • Vendor management • Knowledge of technology standards	• Manages contract • Manages software agreements • Manages warranty agreements • Manages vendor maintenance agreements

Scenarios

Assets newly discovered scenario

I advise that you have a report or alert notification sent to you if new assets are discovered in your ITAM/SAM system that you realized, you have not gone through the proper channels. For instance, a new software application/vendor has been introduced that you and your SAM team were never privy to and had not gone through your software approval process. You would go and research where the software came from, how it was approved, does it meet the company technology and security standards. You would then go and communicate this with the management, an architecture review board if one exists in your organization, and decide how to address this.

Having automated alerts or reports sent to you based on this criteria will allow you to review your inventory info either on a monthly or quarterly basis. However, this assures you that for inventory matters, which need to be addressed immediately, you will receive acknowledgements immediately when something new is discovered, which don't meet the parameters or criteria you have set up. This will allow you to address the issue sooner, rather than later.

The following is an example of asset discovery process:

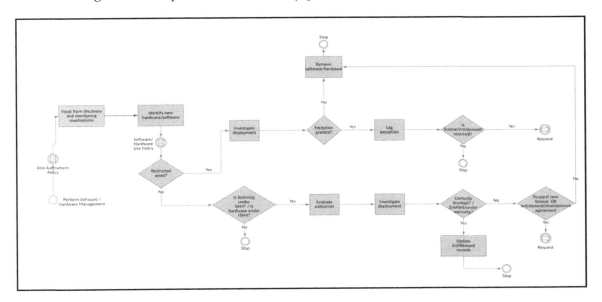

Asset discovery process

The following is an example of the user request and approval process:

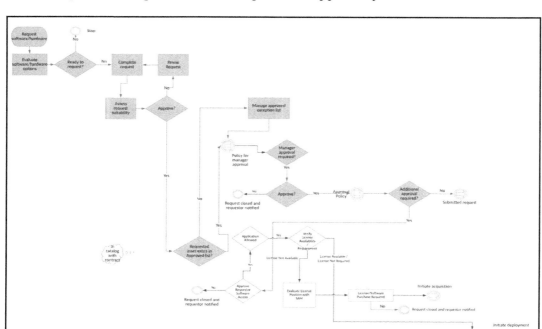

User request and approval process

I'd also like you to walk through how to understand and address unplanned events. When you don't have good control or are not proactive with your program, it can cause all kinds of upheaval and havoc when unplanned situations arise like audits or security vulnerabilities. The following is an example of a high-level flow:

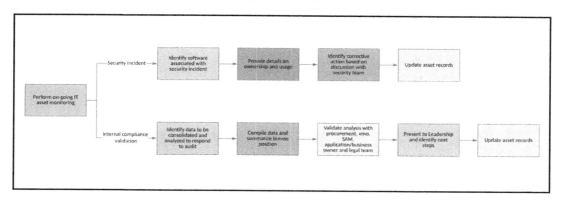

Unplanned event and incident scenario

You've received a request for information. You have received the requests from two internal sources. One request is from your operational team and one is from an application owner. I always advise to ask some key questions, what is the information you are requesting? What do you plan on using it for? When you ask these questions, you will sometimes be surprised by the answer. The responses you receive tell you that a vendor has requested software usage data or a listing of the software products your organization is using.

Now, here comes the fun part. You, SAM, and VMO should enquire with the vendor, if this is possibly an informal audit inquiry. Evaluate request based on contractual audit rights, scope, timeline requirements, and business criticality, and determine whether request should be classified as an audit. If you classify this as an audit, follow the steps and processes from `Chapter 5`, *Understanding and Surviving Software License Compliance Audits*.

Maintain a managed software list scenario

Managing software is hard. Software is hard to pin down. With the ease of electronic access and numerous packaging options for the same software, developing just the list of the software in the environment is hard enough. Add in the complexity of licensing and your SAM program becomes mired down long before reaching compliance. Instead of managing all software the same way and potentially failing, I advise using what I call the **Software Value Risk Analysis (Software VRA™)**, which applies criteria to prioritize your SAM program to minimize the risks of:

- Unplanned financial events
- Poor audit results
- Unsatisfactory service levels

Use your ITAM/SAM system to look at software from every angle, which will help you build a managed software list, a priority list of software where complete management reduces risk the most. Evaluation criteria would be the role of the software within your organization, the total spend and relationship with the vendor, plus information about how the vendors work, and the audit activity. Licensing and strategic IT and organizational goals are essential components of the investigation.

The end result is a new way to look at software exposure, separating software applications into management categories through a calculated level of risk:

Changing the pace

With an inventory of your organization's software, analyze the multiple characteristics that increase risk such as license model, vendor, usage, or type of software. With the value analysis results, your SAM program is refocused on a targeted managed software list. You now have a roadmap to effective risk reduction.

Instead of stopping the creation of the managed software list, also define a strategic software level and identify candidates for a software watch list. Process changes, license model choices, and best practice techniques directed at these applications and vendors will extend the effectiveness of your SAM program.

Software VRA™ real outcomes

Prior to performing the value analysis, the prevailing thought was to track all assets, for all reasons, and to solve all known problems—not an uncommon thought when an ITAM program is initially forming. After the analysis, the potential cost takeout was so compelling that the stakeholders were in lock-step agreement that the program was going to be laser-focused on delivering the agreed-upon value points. Furthermore, the leadership team became genuinely excited about the program. The focus that resulted from the value analysis had the following effects:

1. Instead of tracking all assets, only distributed computers were tracked, since those are the only assets that need to be tracked to deliver on the identified value points.

2. Instead of attempting to apply asset management to data centers, telecom, and the entire enterprise, only the portion of the enterprise where the value existed was addressed. This reduced the scope by half and the complexity by roughly 80%.

3. Instead of all "catch points" (business process points where asset change data is captured) being equally important, the disposal catch point surfaced as the most critical catch point, which translated to a strong program focus on "nailing" that catch point.

4. Instead of having no clearly defined way of evaluating (or pushing back on) change requests, such as requests for new reports, requests for tracking a new class of asset, requests for adding a new field, and many more, the value analysis resulted in a focus by which all change requests could be subsequently compared. For example, how does tracking printers enhance the program's ability to deliver the value statements promised? The focus laid the foundation for a formal ITIL compliant change management system—change management of the ITAM program itself.

5. Instead of the typical high risk of not being able to hold the genuine interest of executives, the value points translated into success metrics, which translated into monthly reporting to executive management on the value being delivered by the program. Now, executive management has been "trained" on what to expect from the program, and when the program delivers, it is, by definition, successful. And since the success metrics are the removal of hard dollar cost, executive interest retention can be expected (as long as the program delivers). Furthermore, since executives see the delivery of the promised value, any gripes they may hear about data accuracy are easily put in perspective.

The bottom line? The program has gained laser focus, full stakeholder support, genuine CIO, and executive-level interest, a means by which the myriad of hallway enhancement requests can be managed, and a way of demonstrating the value that is being produced—a sound platform for success.

What is value analysis and how is it performed? Basically, value analysis is the risk adjusted benefits side of a standard net present value business case. Simply quantify the benefits, adjust for risk, and ignore the cost (initially). Rank the results and focus your ITAM program on the highest points of value. Value points will differ from organization to organization. Usually, the value analysis quantifies what the typical asset manager already knows instinctively. The compelling outcome, however, provides strong justification for holding the line on program focus and measurement, which is essential for success.

Challenges or risks you should anticipate with regards to your program

I wanted to address challenges and risks you should anticipate here. So often, great work gets derailed. I wanted to guide you on what some of these could be and why they happen after you and your enterprise have spent so much time and money to put an ITAM/SAM program in place.

Many organizations implement a tool and do not invest in the planning of the project to support their ITAM/SAM program. I have seen first-hand how risky this point of view can be. If the tool does not have the proper planning, well-defined processes, and enforceable policies in place to support the tool and design a system to ensure your organization complies with the plans and policies, the tool will receive resistance and the organization ends up frustrated and wasting resources.

Another risk is that the people not involved with the development of the ITAM/SAM program and now the tool implementation project may resist the changes because it requires them to do more work or something differently. Communication and promotion of the ITAM/SAM program, and supporting projects, and its benefits is key and will usually manage this risk for you.

Managing the changes that people will want to make after the program and plan is developed can have a huge impact on the assigned resources. To manage this, ensure a change process that includes a team consensus that the change is best for the overall program and not just good for one person by reviewing and attaining approval of the change proposal before implementing the change in the final deliverable. All changes will affect the budgeted resources in one way or another and the program and project team should understand the full impact of the change before accepting it.

Challenges in design come from an unclear vision of the final product. Before leaving the design phase, ensure to not only plan the tool's installation well, but also the tools interface and automated workflows, scripts, and screen designs as well. If the tool is installed and working properly, but if the system is not user friendly or is not logically designed to match the way your organization wants to operate, no one will be happy with the system and the system will never reach its full potential.

Another challenge often comes when you want to report the results of your efforts to management, only to be disappointed when it's discovered that the reporting tool accompanying the selected ITAM/SAM system is limited or not user friendly. Knowing what types of reports are expected and including those expectations in the system planning will prevent disappointment. After all, what good is a great ITAM/SAM system if you cannot get the information required out of the system? As I said in Chapter 6, *ITAM Tools – What Should You Look For?*, do all your homework upfront before making your final decision and big purchase. Have the vendors provided multiple demos to all the various teams within your organization that will be affected in some way by this new change? And, if at all possible, do a **proof-of-concept** (POC) so there are no surprises.

One final risk is to underutilize the tool or attempt to do too much at once. Don't boil the ocean. Either of these can overtax your organization's resources or limit the vision for the ITAM/SAM system, and both will keep the system from growing, improving, and reaching its full potential. Instead, map out the system for a three year span. Each year, develop another portion of the system until it is operating at full potential. For example, year 1 - phase 1: implement basic ITAM/SAM program. Phase 2a: add budgeting and forecasting. Phase 2b - implement an ITAM/SAM tool. Year 2: implement a full chargeback system. Year 3: examine what has changed and improve it.

Summary

ITAM isn't exciting, but ITAM people are!

How you ask? Well...

Isn't intellection exciting?

ITAM brings smart processes to all areas of an organization to interface and bridge the gap between operational and financial divisions, groups, and systems.

Isn't intrigue exciting?

ITAM uncovers the low-hanging fruit and allows you to get to the end result, which will enable your organization to make money, save money, and stay in compliance.

Isn't being undercover exciting?

ITAM is behind the scenes tying everything together through best practices, guidance, and centralized systems in order to ensure financial, risk, and productivity management.

Isn't support exciting?

ITAM provides support through people, practicality, and performance.

Isn't mystery exciting?

ITAM is misunderstood. Because a lot of people don't understand ITAM, they find it perplexing; ITAM people simplify the complex though straightforward policy and processes that are easy to implement and sustain.

Isn't speed exciting?

ITAM allows you to have fast access to the information you need to do your day-to-day functions though centralized, integrated systems.

Isn't being a player exciting?

ITAM allows you to be part of the team that works together to achieve true Enterprise Asset Management. ITAM isn't being on the sidelines, keeping your own spreadsheets, and not passing the information doesn't make you a playmaker. It takes team players to be centralized to benefit the entire organization financially and legally.

Isn't heat exciting?

ITAM is a *hot* program, read more each month in my blog; I will divulge the Intrigue, uncover the mystery, expose the hidden, and give so much more about ITAM and SAM for all you exciting ITAM people.

Made in the USA
Columbia, SC
03 August 2020